T0080921

Tasting Spain

Tasting Spain

A Culinary Tour

by
H M van den Brink

Translated by Yne Hogetoorn

 ArmchairTraveller

First published in Great Britain in 2006 by Haus Publishing Ltd
70 Cadogan Place, London SW1X 9AH

This first paperback edition published in 2016

First published in German as *Spanien mit Leib und Seele: Oasen für die Sinne* by HM van den Brink
© Sanssouci im Carl Hanser Verlag München Wien 2003

Translation copyright © 2006 Yne Hogetoom

The moral rights of the author have been asserted.

A CIP catalogue record for this book is available from the British Library

ISBN 978-1-909961-27-2

Typeset in Garamond by MacGuru Ltd

Printed in Spain

Jacket image: akg-images / Album / Kurwenal / Prisma

www.hauspublishing.com
@HausPublishing

A word in advance

This is not a cookbook. It's a book about eating – about meals I have eaten in Spain, alone or in company, and about my memories of them. These memories were my sole guide while writing: any meal that was still vivid to me after all these years must have been something special.

A cook, a historian or a restaurant critic would follow a less idiosyncratic policy and write a more balanced and practical book about Spanish cuisine. But I am not a cook, nor a historian, nor a critic. I am just an eater.

I am not a Spaniard either. So these memories are just as much about travelling as about eating. Or, to put it more precisely, about leaving and arriving. The urge to leave and the desire to come home belong together, and perhaps mean the same thing, at least to me.

Dutch genre painters of the 17th and 18th centuries painted a scene, often called simply 'Traveller at an inn', which never fails to move me. It is morning and the horses have been saddled – or evening and the luggage is being taken from their backs. The travellers are wearing coats and sometimes a sword or a musket, because they are in unknown surroundings and they must be prepared for any dangers lurking on the road. But this scene, this moment is always peaceful. They have reached a pause in their journey. The inn has a low roof and a hanging sign.

The door is open. The travellers will have to pay for the innkeeper's hospitality, but that is not really important. All that matters is that there is a table under that roof, food and drink are being served on the table and, for a short period of time, the traveller is at home in a world that is usually foreign to him.

Looking back, I think that my memories of meals in Madrid, Barcelona and Teverga are mostly about the feeling of being at home.

I.

The innards of Madrid

1

We lived in Madrid. We lived in Madrid for four years, in a large flat on the third floor of a building in the centre of the city, not far from the Parque del Buen Retiro. Its address was our address, its street was our street, and Moisés, the caretaker with his grey uniform, sitting in his cubby-hole like a clerk at a counter, was our caretaker. Every day we read a Spanish newspaper, and the news in it mattered to us. We went to the bakery, the market and the butcher. We were recognised and were allowed to complain about the weather and about how expensive the peseta had become. The peseta still existed and was expensive during the time we lived in Spain. The weather was always either too hot or too cold.

We lived in Madrid. But we were people who had recently arrived and would leave again one day, so everyday life had the sheen of the unusual, a sheen born of our longing not to feel like strangers but at home – born, in other words, of our lack, our sense that we were guests and had no right to anything. The years I harboured this longing inside me, day after day, lie far behind me. They have become memories, very personal to me, yet I could not say what exactly they consist of – a shape, a sound, a colour, a taste? Or all of these, bound mysteriously together? Sometimes I think I have found the answer to these questions and I feel as if I could hold them in my hand – at other times my certainty is gone and my vivid phrases melt away.

Moisés lived with his family in a small flat in the inner courtyard of the building. In the summer he watered the plants, a battalion of ficuses and cactuses lined up in a square on the paving stones in front of his door. In winter he stoked up the boilers in the basement. He took care that the dustbins were wheeled out and wheeled back in, sorted the post, dividing up the letters and parcels into stacks ready for the residents, and was in general such a whirl of helpful activity that he cast over all his actions the appearance of being absolutely essential.

When I used to leave the building in the morning, Moisés had already finished an important part of his daily routine and was busy polishing the banister. It was made of copper and wound its way through the entire building, from the basement up to the seventh floor. Hardly anyone used the staircase. The residents used the elevator with the beautiful wooden door in the hallway – Moisés jumped out of his cubby hole to push the elevator button for you – and the staff used the one with the metal doors in the inner courtyard. The staircase was dark and looked as if it could do with a fresh coat of paint, but the banister shone like a bright ray of light in the gloom of the high stairwell.

While he was polishing Moisés wore a pale blue overall, but when he had finished, halfway through the morning,

4

he changed into his grey suit, white shirt and black tie. Thus attired he took up his position in front of the house, small and sturdy, his hands behind his back, and greeted in his loud voice whoever went in or out. We always felt rather as if we were being inspected. We knew that there were *porteros* in front of the other buildings on the street and their status depended not only on an impeccably swept doorstep but also on the quality of the residents who used that doorstep, on their behaviour, their status, the family they belonged to, dead ancestors included, the shops they shopped in, the way they dressed – and we failed hopelessly in all these areas, especially the last. The caretakers talked about us, we were certain of that, all the more so because many of them were related. We never knew what they said. But they turned a blind eye to us, at least we hoped so, simply because we were foreigners and no one needs to take foreigners completely seriously. Our handicap had its advantages.

2

I love to breakfast out of doors, preferably on my own. A normal day turns into a holiday if I start it with this small present to myself. At home or in a hotel I do not care so much for breakfast; it takes too long and I am never really hungry. I do not care for holidays either for that matter; one day without work is a day where a sense of uselessness soon takes over. But when I can start a new morning in peace, when I have walked a few steps outside my door and enjoyed the small cocktail of luxury, anonymity and theatre that is the essence of visiting a restaurant or café, then I am as bright and fit as other people are after a week on the beach. Breakfast out of doors tastes of freedom. You are pleasantly detached from it all.

I stepped out of the elevator and greeted the polishing Moisés who greeted me back and laughed in such an exuberant manner that it looked as if he had seen something odd about me – which of course was true. He believed I was going to work. But I was only going around the corner to sit with my newspaper at the bar of a big café with imitation marble and brass-framed smoked-glass mirrors, a style of décor to which all the modern bars and restaurants in Spain have fallen victim – it's regrettable, but I can put up with it.

Most of the early customers had left the café long ago, as the crumbs of food, sachets of sugar and cigarette ends on the floor testified. Hundreds of cups of coffee and dozens of beers or glasses of *sol-y-sombra* had already been served. This deadly mix of aniseed liqueur and Spanish cognac had been served to people on their way to serious jobs, unlike mine, for which they required, it seemed, a hefty dose of encouragement. I ordered a coffee with milk. Not a cappuccino – that affected drink with its meringue of milk so light that it can lie on top of the coffee (where it instantly turns cold) and which is, on top of that, often sprinkled with cocoa as if you were in a cake shop. Fortunately, this Italian nonsense has few supporters in Spain. Coffee has to be strong, should come from a machine making lots of noise, and has to be served as soon as the final drop has landed in the cup. Only then should the waiter appear with two cans of milk, milk that foams but does not consist entirely of foam, to ask if you would prefer hot or lukewarm milk. Hot please. The waiter pours the milk from one of the shining metal cans. Hot, but not boiling hot. There has to be a fair share of black and white, so that the *mestizaje* does justice to both of them. It is *café con leche* that should really be called 'sun-and-shadow'. I ordered a coffee and something to eat.

Breakfast is the most neglected meal in Spanish cuisine – which is actually saying too much already, because 'to neglect' sounds like an activity, an active attitude, and in the morning most Spanish people are not occupied with anything that looks like the consuming of a meal. Consequently, there is not a lot of choice in most cafés in the first hours of the morning: gooey cakes that keep for months on end, iced cakes that stick to the teeth, vac-uum-packed *bollos* from the bread factory – the Spanish will eat anything so long as it keeps the blood sugar level high and the energy running till two o'clock in the after-noon. It is no surprise that by that time you badly need something substantial, the most important hot meal of the day.

If you are lucky – and you do not have to worry too much about having a healthy start to your day – you live near a *churros* bakery. There was one close to our house: a small niche of a shop with a gigantic kettle of oil stood on a stove, into which the stallholders squeeze long circles of dough out of the star nozzle of a piping bag. The result is a thin (*churro*) or a thick (*porra*) brown string, which prob-ably comes closest to the Dutch *oliebol* (a kind of dough-nut), but is less chewy, as there is less soft part and more crust. Eaten immediately, hot, they are like most sins: no less sinful in the heat of the moment than considered in hindsight, and in any case irresistible. You sprinkle sugar on top, which melts at once, and sip coffee between each bite. Alternatively, you dunk the crispy circle shamelessly in your cup.

You are seldom so lucky. The small shop on our corner was run by two men whose faces through the long years had taken on the colour of the weak dough they were mixing. Or perhaps their natural complexion influenced their choice of career, though that seems a little less likely. From early morning onwards they were bent over their smoking kettles. The same kettles in which they fried potato chips in the afternoon, and in the same oil, I am afraid. After I had bought my bag of *churros* I would race back home with my purchase clasped under my coat, but by the time the *churros* appeared on our table they would already be too cold. Better to eat them close to the place where they are prepared. *Churros* and *porras* are often made on squares and street corners. At break of dawn after a long night in Madrid, accompanied by a cup of hot chocolate, they are the traditional hangover breakfast of late revellers. Sometimes you can get *churros* in cafés, where they usually lie a little sadly on a plate under a glass case having turned cold and hard, hardly edible as they are and even worse when they are put in the microwave. No one seems to mind. The sticky dough continues to sell, well into the afternoon.

So there is a lot to be said against *churros*. Then again, my first introduction to them was nothing short of an epiphany, perhaps the first time I realised that, for me, something special was hidden precisely in Spain's imperfections, something to do with me, but not actually me – although I am sure at the time I did not understand it like that. It was my first journey across Spain's plateau. An unwashed morning after a sleepless night at a guesthouse in an ugly village, but not so ugly that I can remember the name. In the thin air voices sounded like shiny tools. The cold cut through my two jumpers. A bus was droning, waiting to leave, though no one knew exactly when. The black smoke from the exhaust pipe hovered above the pavement of the village square and then drifted upwards to lose itself in the immense winter sky. And in a corner of this square stood a flaming burner and a big black pan in which the snakes of pale dough were hissing and twisting in concentric circles, changing colour until, golden brown, they were fished out with a wooden skimmer, cut into pieces, sprinkled with sugar and handed to the customer in a bag made of newspaper. The fat left big dark spots on the paper and made the articles in the *El Adelanto* or *La Voz de Castilia* unreadable. My first bite into the crispy dough was so good it almost hurt. Ever since, I have associated *churros* with cold and headaches. They don't cure headaches, but they offer more comfort than an aspirin – and comfort is more important than the absence of pain.

Churros

about 16 pieces
475 ml water
1 tsp salt

250 g flour
oil
sugar to sprinkle

*Bring the water to the boil in a pan with the salt
and a squeeze of oil. Add all the flour, and stir
double-quickly with a wooden spoon till a large
dough ball is formed. Leave to cool a little. Fill a
piping bag with a 5 mm nozzle with the dough,
and squeeze out in pieces about 10 cm long into a
saucepan containing a large amount of hot vegetable
oil. Fry around 4* churros *at a time, turning them
when they are golden brown. In* Churrerías *they are
usually fried in large round circles, after which they
are cut to measure. Let them drain on kitchen paper
and serve warm, with sugar.*

3

Luckily, I usually breakfasted late in Madrid, because
the kitchens in most cafés and restaurants get started
between nine and ten and one of the first things they
make is the *tortilla*. By the time I arrived it was already on
the counter, a big yellow slice, still steaming and sparkling
with little drops of oil. Not the *tortilla francesa*, which is
just an omelette, but the *tortilla española*, whose main
ingredients are eggs and potatoes. It is a very simple dish,
but like all simple dishes it requires precision. Not only
must the ingredients be in exactly the right proportions,
but the heat of the pan and the duration of frying need to
be carefully controlled.

You should suppress your impatience for a while after the plate of *tortilla* has been placed on the counter, because it is one of those dishes that is best neither hot nor cold but lukewarm. Delaying heightens the pleasure. Have a look around, read something, take a sip of coffee and then place your order: *tortilla* on bread. Most Spanish people prefer no more than a small piece of bread next to their *pincho de tortilla*, the snack they sometimes put away at eleven o'clock in order to make the long trek to lunch more bearable. But I am having breakfast. For me it is only when the *tortilla* is wrapped in a piece of baguette and shoved into my mouth that I experience that perfect, dreamed-of first bite, a series of revelations one inside the other: first the hard crust of the bread, then the tender crumb, after that the surface of the *tortilla* which in its turn bursts open to release the soft, almost fluid innermost part, with its slight accents of salt and onion. You experience this taste sensation twice over, in a kind of mixed-up stereo, because a human being has two lips and two rows of teeth and a tongue that mediates between the upper and lower parts while the jaws grind and chew. The mouth is a perfect instrument. Now some coffee quickly and then the second bite, because desire wants eternity and in the world of mortals there is no other eternity than repetition.

Bread and potatoes, eggs and oil. It seems like a strange, heavy combination to start the day with but it is the most beautiful breakfast I know, strong and delicate at the same time, both in taste and texture, and furthermore it has the effect that as far as food is concerned

I do not need anything else for hours to come. I could, if I wanted, remain a foreigner and ignore the Spanish lunch. In Madrid I seldom breakfasted any other way. I do not like change very much. I only want a new newspaper every day – and even with that, you do wonder how much of each article offers new knowledge or observation and how much is just ritual.

I do not like change very much and that is exactly why an exception to the rule makes a special impression on me. I was once sitting in a café in Bilbao where by ten o'clock the staff were passing one *tortilla* variation after the other from the kitchen and placing it on the counter. The waitress, perhaps out of a benign form of Basque nationalism – one of the few – did not want to give me a simple Spanish *tortilla*. I had to try something else, at her risk: *tortilla* with stockfish. Fish in the morning. Just the thought of it was ... But it was a strange, smoky but fresh dish, which tasted of fish and then again did not, and in the end I could only be grateful for the girl's persistence. It did not make me change my breakfast preference but it did persuade me to think differently about Bilbao thereafter, to recall, along with the gloomy harbours in winter and the absurd spaceship of the Guggenheim museum, the taste of stockfish and to remember the smile of a waitress about whom I have forgotten everything else – her voice, the colour of her hair, the colour of her eyes.

Tortilla Española
Spanish Omelette
There is no onion in the classic tortilla de patatas

(potato omelette), but the omelette is better with it.
The number of eggs and potatoes you use depends
on the size of your frying pan. The recipe below is for
a frying pan with a diameter of 25 cm, preferably
with a high, vertical side. The common mistake
that many non-Spaniards make when preparing
the tortilla *is with the quantity of olive oil. In order*
for the potatoes to be done they need to be fried in
a large amount of oil, so that they are more or less
covered by it. When they are done, carefully pour off
the oil to use again later.

2 servings
750 g potatoes
1 small onion
salt
6 eggs
olive oil

Peel the uncooked potatoes, cut into thin slices and
sprinkle with salt. Chop up the onion finely. Heat
the olive oil in a frying pan and gently fry the
potatoes and onion for about 15 minutes, until they
are done. Stir with a wooden spoon. Be careful: do
not let the potatoes turn golden brown! Meanwhile
beat six eggs in a large bowl. When the potatoes
are done, pour off the oil and add the mixture of
potatoes and onion to the eggs. Stir well and leave to
cool. Heat the olive oil in a clean pan over medium
heat, and then pour the contents of the bowl into

the pan. When the bottom is set, turn the tortilla with the help of a large plate or lid. The tortilla can be eaten well done, or not completely set, so that the middle springs back a little when you press it. The tortilla tastes best lukewarm. With a fresh salad, baguette and red wine it makes an ideal lunch.

Stuffed tortilla can be made in two ways: either you fry the filling with it, or you make an extra thick, well-fried tortilla de patatas, cut it in half with a bread knife and fill it with, for example, spinach or mayonnaise, tomatoes and tuna-fish or chicken.

Stewed spinach with garlic, green asparagus tips or wild mushrooms are successful fillings for frying with the potatoes.

Tortilla con Bacalao
Stockfish Omelette

Bacalao, stockfish, is actually salted cod. The bacalao sold in Turkish or Moroccan shops is often made of ling, a fish that has less taste than cod. In Spanish and Portuguese shops they sell bacalao made of cod. This fish has to be de-salted in ample water, which should be changed twice.

2 servings
100 g boneless bacalao in cubes
100 g finely chopped onion
olive oil (extra virgin)
6 eggs

a pinch of cayenne pepper
salt
2 tbsp finely chopped parsley

Heat three tablespoons of olive oil in a frying pan and fry the onion and the fish over a low heat for about 15 minutes or till the fish is done. Place the mixture on a plate and mash with a fork. Beat the eggs together with 1 tablespoon of water, add salt, parsley and cayenne to taste, then add the fish mixture. Stir briefly. Heat some more oil in the pan and pour everything in it. Simmer gently till it is done. After about 10 minutes put the lid on the pan so that the top sets as well. Turn the omelette with the help of a plate or a lid and briefly fry the other side. Serve at room temperature.

4

I wonder whether a taste can travel, across the world and through time. I doubt it, though I know my doubt makes little sense. A skilled cook can make anything over and over again anywhere: that is what recipes are for. Refrigerated transport delivers the ingredients. So it is probably because I am not a cook, but an eater, because I am someone who wants to be a guest, arrive home like the Prodigal Son for whom the fatted calf is slaughtered, that I prefer to connect a special taste with a place, a city, a region, a country; and with a certain time, particular weather, a season. I do not feel the need to breakfast on *tortilla* outside Spain, even though it would be possible to do so. Justa, Moisés' wife, gave us the recipe and showed us how to do it. But if I were to take that perfect bite of *tortilla* in London, Berlin or Amsterdam, I would miss the dirty floor, the façades of the buildings and Madrid's silvery Velázquez light. I know very well that it is possible to eat fresh strawberries in December – but I do not see the attraction of that either. Others may experience it as a pleasant luxury, a form of wealth, the availability and accessibility of everything. But not to be able to be where you really are and not to be able to wait, not to be able to long for what is temporarily or forever unattainable ... I find that rather insipid and miserable. For me, a life without lack would be like giving up on an essential spice, or the taste of salt or oil. Perhaps I am better at arriving than at travelling.

∽

Ever since Marcel Proust brought a spoonful of tea with biscuit crumbs to his mouth and thought he found his lost youth again, it has become a commonplace that taste and scent are carriers of memories. By logical extension, perhaps the right recipe could bring back to life an entire past. As if the memory had been kept inside, like a face on a photograph you can take out any time you please, or music on a CD. But it is not that simple. Not in real life and not even with Proust.

Inside that 'almost unreal, small' drop of tea, as Proust writes at the end of the famous first chapter of *A la récherche du temps perdu*, 'the immense building of memories' had been preserved 'intact'. The 'wandering souls' of taste and smell rediscover their 'old past' in that house and bring it back to life. But what exactly do they find? Proust, usually such a master of the precise formulation, shaped to eliminate all uncertainty, contradicts himself here. This cup of tea has not preserved his entire youth in Combray, all the flowers, the houses, the church and the people. Nor do its taste and smell have power over the past, no more than his memory does, which he portrays, at first, as quite passive.

It is, rather, the combination of these elements that starts the building process. The raw materials, naturally, are the memories; taste and smell are the architects and the contents of the teacup act as a catalyst, or, to continue the architectural metaphor, as the cement. This catalyst or cement itself consists of two elements: the tea and the madeleine biscuit. Separately they mean nothing and for someone else, someone other than Marcel Proust, without his memories and his sensitive and intelligent mind, they would not bring about the same sensation. It is something 'inside me', the narrator acknowledges soon after the first sip, that has filled him with a joy he cannot explain. To his horror he notices that the effect diminishes with each following sip. It takes hard work to recreate the sensation without it evaporating instantly. But this is what Proust does, over many years of his life and thousands of pages. This first moment, which is often incorrectly linked to the taking of a bite from the madeleine biscuit, does not produce an immediate or complete revelation. For Proust smell and taste cannot be pinned down either in memory or in food and drink. They come into being only in the connection *between* mind and matter and the effort to remember.

This thought may be scientifically dubious, but I like it very much. Now that everything else, every movement and every sound, can be recorded and endlessly reproduced on discs and tapes, films and photographs, taste and smell are the last wandering souls. The meal is an intangible experience which can only be experienced again by recreating it, by repeating the creation and even pure repetition is not good enough, more is needed: the right people and the right spot and a mind receptive to the effect. Each meal is also a memory of all previous meals. Good cooks have to be masters of repetition. If only writers' painful efforts at originality could produce a similar effect.

So that is how it came about that I breakfasted hundreds of times in Spain with the same coffee and the same *tortilla*, while reading the news, which was really of little concern to me, poring over local political scandals, which I knew I would not be able to repeat a week later, looking around me, at the light that fell on the dirty floor, that played on the façades of the buildings outside, at the passers-by – not at the ugliness or at the beauty but at the unreality of it all, an unreality of my own devising, because I had no part in this world and so did not have to express an opinion, as if it were a story I had put in a frame and made into a play. But why did I enjoy this feeling so much in Spain of all places, and not in France or in Italy, for example? Why here particularly, in this country whose language I did not even speak properly?

5

Madrid is the capital of a small land mass containing a great variety of landscapes, languages, peoples and climates. Madrid is the New York of Spain, a large part of the inhabitants was not born there, people move to the city from all over the country, to the metropolis, to the factories, the art, the politics, the money, the intoxication of the big life. But, unlike most New Yorkers, the people of Madrid do not want to forget their place of origin. They are proud to be living in the capital and materially speaking they are usually better off than in the village where they or their parents were born. But there is also *mi tierra*, not only the mythical place of origin but also often very concretely the place where the family still owns a piece of land, a house, sometimes barely fit to live in but even so, an excuse to hold on to the dream that someday they will return for good to where they originally came from, even if there are all sorts of practical objections that ensure they never do.

This love for the native soil is the reason why hundreds of villages in the Spanish countryside, which are populated by just a handful of poor elderly people in winter, come back to life for four weeks in August. Garlands hang in the main street; garden chairs stand amongst the tall, overgrown grass. Classmates who have been scattered all over the world for decades polish up memories on the benches of a school whose roof has long since collapsed, family quarrels whose origin has been forgotten are enthusiastically revived, cars growl, children shout and everyone eats and drinks late into the warm night.

During the holidays you do not go abroad. You go back home.

In September it is quiet again in the villages and life in Madrid resumes its normal course. City life is completely different from that month in the village, except for one thing: the food. Madrid doesn't really have its own cuisine. Madrid is first and foremost the sum of all those farm villages. The present city-dwellers have brought the recipes with them from their own region, or from their parents' or grand-parents' region. They have added something, they have probably tried something from their neighbours, they have profited from wider choice and increased prosperity – but back in their flats they remain the children of the arid earth in that sad village.

What goes for the kitchen at home also goes for eating out. In Madrid you can get the best food from Andalusia and Extremadura, even the Basque and Catalan restaurants are not bad, and for hundreds of years they have prided themselves on the quality of their fresh seafood, the crustaceans and shellfish, which used to be supplied in casks filled with sea water on the backs of mules and nowadays are transported in lorries driving day and night, their refrigerator units humming and rumbling. Of course this variety, this choice of the best from all the provinces, contributes to the attraction the capital holds for the rest of the country. But still I suspect that all these different regional restaurants have for a long time been of more interest to people looking for something familiar than to those seeking something new. This discovery surprised me.

In my youth, visiting a restaurant was a special event, almost always associated with an essential celebration or a distant journey. There were not many restaurants in the Netherlands in the 1960s. For ordinary people eating out meant going to a Chinese. There you could get what you did not get at home – and that was mainly the point. Why would you go out for something and pay expensive prices for it if you could make it yourself?

Life in northern Europe has become less housebound, more Mediterranean the past 30 years, it has acquired a looseness that does not always look good on us. But even though the number of times we visit a restaurant has increased, we still go out to experience something special, something new, an exotic sensation. It is different in Spain, which, according to a statistic I am unable to verify, has more restaurants than all the other countries in Western Europe put together. The greatest compliment I have heard Spanish friends pay the waiters and cooks is that the food was just as good as every previous time. And sometimes even that it matched the food as it used to be, back home. In all the larger Spanish cities, and in Latin America too, you will find cultural centres for immigrants from Galicia, Asturias, Andalusia, La Rioja. I doubt that there is a great deal of poetry being read or theatre performed. But you can always eat. In Spain they seem to understand Proust.

My own youth was poor in tastes. I was born where the Rhine flows lazily into the North Sea, near a Dutch town with stately canals and dead straight alleyways. The first dish that spontaneously comes to my mind is the *hutspot* (stew), which was traditionally made every year on 3 October. On this date in 1574 the city was liberated from a Spanish siege that had lasted for months. Legend has it that a boy came across the Spanish positions, which had been hurriedly abandoned after the Geuzen rebels had pierced the dikes, and brought back a pot of food to the hungry population. You can still admire the pot in the town museum. No one knows what exactly was inside but people assume it was one of the countless variations on *olla podrida*, the 'powerful pot' in which meat, sausage and fat are slowly cooked with the available vegetables over a low fire. The Dutch version is a heavy stew of potatoes, carrots and onions served with brisket of beef. Once a year our house smelled of simmering meat and onions from the early morning onwards. There was a fairground in town at the same time.

But other than that? The *slavink* (rolls of mincemeat wrapped in bacon)? Fish fingers? Wednesday minced meat day? *Smac* (spam)? I am afraid that my native region has for a long time had few traditional dishes and that what there was disappeared by the middle of the last century because of the austerity of the post-war period, commercial pressures and a lack of interest. Especially the last, I think. Or do I perhaps not *want* to remember anything of my home? The tastes that did make a lasting impression on me are connected with a different house, my grandmother's, which stood further upstream, in Germany, on a hill with a view over the Rhine. The Rhine always seemed to be in a hurry, swirling and foaming and bursting its banks at the end of each winter. I remember the venison goulash. I remember the veal with mushrooms and raisins. I remember the French beans we picked together; the long rows of jam jars in the basement; I remember the fresh salad, which my Grandmother dressed with sugar; bread and tomatoes sprinkled with chopped onions and parsley; I remember the gooseberries and the mirabelle plums with the cream she whipped with her lean hard hands and which tasted sweeter than anywhere else. A festively laid table awaited us when we arrived after our long journey in a warm and sticky train. We were encouraged to eat well, because we needed to recover our strength and of course to grow, but more importantly because, as she put it, in a saying I understood only much later, 'Food keeps body and soul together'. I heard my grandmother say this hundreds of times, my grandmother who had lived through two world wars and had lost her brothers in the first and her husband after the second. It was not a cajoling suggestion; it was a moral imperative. The saying even had a religious tone; my grandmother was a devout Catholic. Two or three weeks a year during the summer holidays I tasted a life I was related to, but which I could not call mine. The Dutch and the Germans do not have much in common and I did not really feel at home in either country. Perhaps I am not even good at arriving, only at longing for it.

⌐

In the summertime, like everyone else, Moisés and Justa exchanged the city for the country. Their piece of land lies southeast of Madrid, in the poor area between Cuenca and Albacete. Their village is called Las Pedroneras. I have never been there. I only know it owes its fame to its probably self-conferred title as the 'capital of garlic'. It does not have any significant attractions, but Las Pedroneras undeniably lies in the middle of garlic fields, where at harvest time the garlic is picked and processed at high speed, and there are garlic traditions and garlic festivals and markets for the garlic trade. The harvest amounts to 60 million kilos a year. Impossible, it seems to me, to grow up there and not have distinctive memories of smell and taste.

Upon their return to Madrid the couple presented us with a bundle of garlic of striking proportions – at our usual rate of consumption certainly enough for two to three years. The presentation was accompanied by a great deal of laughter as usual, but also by a cordiality that touched us. A little later we were left staring speechless at the bundle of pink-white bulbs. We hung it next to the kitchen window. What could we do with it? It wouldn't be right for this foodstuff to end up as mere decoration. But what then? We were surely not the only ones to wrestle with this problem. They must have ways of dealing with their surplus in Las Pedroneras as well. Sixty million kilos ... We made a Castilian garlic soup, which, as well as garlic, contains bread and eggs and also meat leftovers, if you can find any. A poor person's dish: fuel for a body that has to endure work in the heat or cold. It had a strong, creamy taste and we thanked Justa and Moisés because, for a moment, our flat had smelled of their summer.

Hutspot
Stew with Rib of Beef

4 servings
400 g rib of beef
250 g onions, chopped into rings
1 kg potatoes, peeled and chopped
750 g carrots, scrubbed and diced
salt and pepper

Simmer the rib of beef in a litre of water over a low heat for an hour and a half. Then add the chopped onion rings, the peeled and chopped potatoes and the scrubbed and diced carrots. Add salt to taste. Allow to simmer for another 30 minutes till the vegetables are done. Remove the meat from the pan and slice it. Drain the vegetables, mash them, season with freshly ground pepper, and perhaps a knob of butter. Serve together with the meat on a preheated dish.

Sopa de Ajos
Garlic Soup from Castilia
In its simplest version this soup was made from little more than bread, water, oil, garlic and salt. Fortunately, nowadays you can use stock instead of water.

4 servings
4 large garlic cloves
olive oil
4 slices of (old) baguette

1 tbsp of mild paprika
1 litre beef stock
salt
4 eggs

Heat some oil in a pan, preferably of Spanish earthenware. Fry the clove of garlic whole and the bread till golden brown, then remove both from the pan. Take the pan off the stove and add the paprika to the oil, stirring well. Crush the garlic with a fork and stir through the oil and paprika mixture. Add the pieces of bread and the stock, flavour with salt and pepper and allow to boil over a low heat for 20 minutes. Then carefully break four eggs into the soup, and boil them, with the lid on the pan, for 3 minutes. Alternatively, you can pour the soup into 4 earthenware bowls, break an egg over each of them and put them for 10 minutes into a preheated oven at 200° C until the eggs are set.

6

At the far end of the stately Paseo del Prado lies the railway station, where trains have arrived from the East and the South ever since the 19th century. Stations dating from that period look like cathedrals, but in place of the names of saints, they proudly announce the distant destinations at the other end of the iron way. 'Alicante' and 'Zaragoza' it says on the baroque brick façade of Atocha station. Some clever structural modifications to accompany the inauguration of the high-speed train to Seville have given the station the air of an airport. The 18th-century building directly opposite, once a hospital, now the Reina Sofia museum for modern art, has had a similar makeover. But neither the hi-tech architecture, nor the art bookshops and shops selling arty T-shirts and post-cards, have essentially changed the character of the area. In most respects it remains dominated by the railway, a no man's land of farewell and arrival, haste and fatigue, sorrow and expectation, the grey and grimy strip that lies between the railway and the centre in every big city, like the band of wreckage and spume between the beach and the sea.

The areas around stations always look the same. Something of the grandeur of travelling in former days is often still visible, but covered with a crust of dust and fractured paint, and surrounded by ugly, botched commercial buildings. Everywhere are the same screaming neon signs, the same cheap shops and probably the same pickpockets, masters of an international language of gesture. The resolute pace of the travellers contrasts with the sad look of the permanent street-dwellers, who hardly move: beggars and junkies, street-traders and prophets. And always many foreign faces, nowadays usually from Africa, as if the vicinity of departing trains makes the homesickness more bearable. I like walking through these neighbour-hoods. The ugliness makes me angry but I am also irre-sistibly tempted by all the promises, even though I know they will be false.

In the area surrounding stations there is almost always a red-light district – and that is also probably meant to fight off homesickness, or a kind of homesickness. But whereas Amsterdam or Frankfurt emphasise the display and praise of human flesh, Madrid lures you with pork. Just look at the row of cafés directly opposite Atocha station. Look in the shop window, the largest of its kind, not without reason adorned with the name El Brillante. Inside are heaps of meat and entrails: besides the entire piglets cut open, there are steaks and meat on skewers, there are ears and snouts and trotters, trays filled with liver, with thymus glands, with tripe, with brains and entrails wrapped around sticks. There are sausages in all shapes and sizes: bright red *chorizos* from Pamplona, pale *butifarra* from Catalonia, black pudding from Burgos, which is seasoned with aniseed and filled with rice. And above this quivering landscape hangs a thick curtain of dried ham, pigs' hind legs, with the small, cloven hoofs still on them. Of course there are also beef and the inevitable squid rings. But the produce of the friendly curly-tail predominates. It is an impressive tableau.

Suddenly it is not that difficult to imagine what that poor immigrant from the provinces is thinking, standing in front of such a shop-window, cardboard suitcase in his hand. He is thinking: this must be paradise. He has not come to Madrid to have adventures, but to fill his stomach. He does not want something *different*, he wants *more*. Until the 1950s, people starved in Spain; children died in the countryside after a crop failure or just because of lack of money. The traveller has known this hunger and now he is standing in front of this window and sees the obscene abundance, this wealth of meat. It is as if the

28

whole of Spain offers itself to him here, yields itself, and not quietly, but in eager disarray, inside out, ripped open, dissected, so that everything is visible, the intestines, the ribs, the other organs. And everything at a reasonable price. With pounding hearts we stepped inside, the immigrant and I. It was exciting, but it was a little scary at the same time.

The dining-hall of El Brillante is a large, tiled room; on the right-hand side a counter runs the entire length of the room. Behind it stood men in white coats who, in spite of their heavy build, filled glasses and served helpings of food at a surprising speed. They spoke curtly; they were impatient. There were signs to recommend the specialities. There were so many signs that it seemed almost everything was a speciality. The list of available dishes was very long but most of the food had been prepared in the kitchens beforehand, which were probably located in the basement. Whenever someone placed an order that had to be fried or grilled on the spot, a white coat shouted to the opposite side of the restaurant, where two heavily sweating colleagues were in charge of the cooking. The cooks shouted back when the desired dish was ready or they shuffled over to the counter with it. Sometimes the waiter added a little something, a slice of lemon or a piece of pepper before depositing the dish with a bang in front of the customer. It was a very inefficient system but all involved stuck to it stoically and made up for it by working hard. The men already looked very tired but still the mountains of food would not grow smaller. I thought: what would my imaginary traveller order right now? Something that was expensive and he did not know. I asked for a plate of pigs' ears.

The ears must have come from small pigs. They looked hard and crispy, like potato crisps, but my fork pierced them effortlessly. Would they have stayed tender? I was deceived again. Cartilage crunched between my teeth, but it tasted of glue. That is how it felt in my mouth as well. Pieces of ear stuck to my tongue and my palate. It seemed impossible to swallow it all. It needed beer. Bread. And a spicy sauce. Just then it was hard to agree with the Spaniards' proud claim that they can use every part of the pig: the meat, the bones, the skin and even the bristles. What is not fit to be served, which is very little, is ground down and put in fodder or in sausages. Only the eyes may be discarded. I just hope they at least do that.

7

Both the cheapest and the most expensive meat comes from the pig. The most expensive is *jamón serrano*, ham from the indigenous black animals. They ought to have been allowed to walk around freely, in the shade of trees; ideally, they have fed themselves on acorns.

The best *serrano* ham comes from the area around Salamanca, from Granada and from the Extremadura, so it comes from poor areas, even though the ham is a sign of prosperity. Tenants used to have to pay their landlord in hams after slaughtering. The exuberant torero who had risked his life for a few coins showed off his success by travelling from arena to arena with a whole ham in his car, or on his back. The immigrant who can afford a whole ham instead of pigs' ears can say that his plans worked out well.

'Museo del Jamón' is the name of a small chain of shops that specialises in selling and serving this special product. You will find them in various parts of Madrid, and in other cities as well. The word 'museum' suggests a certain pretentiousness – it smells of 'Culture' – but in practice these shops are no less intimidating than El Brillante. The shop windows are hung full of pigs' legs. Large parts of the ceiling are covered by a forest of dark-red and yellowish-brown, low-hanging, white-veined thighs, each provided with a small tray to catch the fluid still dripping from it, so that it does not land on the customers' heads. When you step inside, you are immediately caught by the heavy smell, sweet and strong as if from a strange type of resin, although unmistakably animal as well. It is of course the smell of blood and meat, of life and death wrapped in blankets of white fat. It is a smell that always awakes, at least in me, a hearty appetite.

There is no quick way to remove dried ham from the bone, mechanically or otherwise. After you have ordered you have to wait till someone arrives and, with either great dexterity or a lot of patience, or usually both, slices beautifully thin pieces with a long, sharp knife and drapes them in circles on a plate. It does not seem an enviable job to me, cutting ham in this 'museum' all day; it must be as bad as opening oysters one after the other. Or does it bestow a kind of status? The plate, soon placed in front of the customer, is not only a sign of his or her prosperity. It is also a kind of historic national symbol, a symbol of the wealthy, mighty, united, Catholic Spain after the expulsion of the Jews and the Muslims.

These two communities, which lived peacefully in Spain during the Middle Ages, could hardly interpret El Brillante's window display as anything other than a brutal provocation. The sweet-smelling heaven of the Museo del Jamón would have been like hell to them. After the Catholic kings reconquered Granada and expelled the Jews, they didn't just bring Spain under the sign of the cross. They also established the reign of the pig. *Marrano* means (male) pig, but is also a term of abuse for a Jew who has converted to Christianity. You can expect the strangest things from people who solemnly consume the body of their own Saviour.

Everywhere in the world, even in Spain, pigs have a bad reputation during their lifetime. They eat waste; they root about in the mud. Only after it has died does the animal change into something not only wanted but also honoured. Little is necessary to effect this transubstantiation. Whereas sophisticated Arabic and Jewish cuisines combine tastes and spices, Catholic Spanish cuisine is characterised by simplicity. The most important thing is that the ingredients are fresh and of good quality. This is partly why restaurants display dead animals and even fruit and vegetables in their windows: just having the produce is half the battle, and its presence is enough to convince the public. But I cannot help but think of the gesture with which the priest raises the bread and shows it to the congregation before it changes into flesh, and the wine into blood. Any meal of significance has the character of a sacrifice; it says something about life and death. That is why there is such a thing as forbidden meat, but no forbidden vegetables.

My wait has been rewarded. It is now in front of me: a big white plate of slices of delicately-veined ham, carefully arranged in a circle, a halo, an aureole which is not holy but absolutely earthly because the periphery and the centre are of the same substance. Inside each circle lies a smaller circle until the entire plate is filled, meat surrounded by meat. No garnish. The taste is soft but unmistakable, a little earthy but it does not linger, on the contrary: the fibres that looked so firm are now doing their very best to melt in your mouth. It is nothing more than raw meat, dried in the air, and it requires nothing else. Do not eat any bread with it. No olives. Drink a full-bodied red wine from Toro or Priorato; preferably not sherry, although that is not entirely forbidden.

A plate of ham is the favourite starter in Madrid, a city populated by people that still call themselves Galician or Andalusian, even after generations; a city that sometimes itself looks like an elaborate first course compared to the rest of Spain; a royal residence that has remained the capital of countryside cooking.

8

One day, because I was rich, I booked a table at Lhardy's. Lhardy is the best and the oldest restaurant in Madrid. It has been open without interruption since 1839. It owes its existence to a short-lived interest in French cuisine, to that period which lasted till the end of the 19th century when Spain opened up to the rest of the world – when the big new parts of Madrid were built, the broad avenues, the underground, the parks and the bank buildings. They even created a *madrileño* folklore, with festivals and traditional costume, to make the people so proud of their city that they wouldn't have to think of other places any more. Lhardy owes its survival and its reputation to two classic menu items with nothing of the metropolitan about them: *callos* and *cocido*, tripe and stew. For more than a century and a half Lhardy has been the place where politicians and businessmen plot discretely, where kings dine with their ministers and mistresses, where the best torero celebrates his most beautiful victory with impresarios and large landowners. It is a man's restaurant.

Curious and at the same time a little nervous, I arrived too early, so I was not allowed to go through the discrete door, not yet allowed to enter the hallway nor to climb the stairs, even though the doorman in his stately coat nodded not entirely coldly to me. I looked inside the shop on the ground floor for a moment, where they sell delicacies from their own kitchen, and pastries, typical sweet stuff from Madrid like the *huesos de los santos*, the bones of saints. Pastry with honey, marzipan and sugar is Spain's most important inheritance from Islamic cooking, so it is probably no coincidence that so many sweet delicacies carry the names of saints and that convents have specialised in their production, in order to ensure the Christianisation of the food.

At the back of Lhardy's shop a silver tureen sits on a gas flame all day. Regular customers can help themselves to the nourishing bouillon inside and then hand over the price, which they naturally know by heart. But I was not that self-confident and besides I was shortly to dine in the drawing room on the first floor. My reservation had been accepted! So I walked on, as if I had to take care of something, down the Carrera de San Jerónimo, in the direction of Sol, not even a hundred metres away.

The Puerta del Sol is supposed to be the heart of Spain. Kilometre zero is here and on New Year's Eve a crowd gathers to watch the clock on the city hall to see when exactly the new year starts. Even so it is a peculiar square with no atmosphere, a hole in the city where one or two newspaper stands and a bus stop cannot conceal the emptiness. It is always busy, but mostly with people wanting to cross it as quickly as possible. Everything interesting lies around it. There are a couple of streets where cheap bars and restaurants are packed in next to each other, where you can also buy tickets for the bullfights. Day and night these streets smell of grilled meat and stale wine. The shops selling mass vestments, plaster statues and other devotional objects are also grouped close together, as are the specialist establishments selling knives and scissors, umbrellas and walking sticks, material for ball gowns, hats, and, last but not least, the sellers of buttons and trimmings with their high walls covered with little wooden drawers. They have sought each other out. It is easy to see how the city centre once functioned: it used to be the place where you went once or twice a year to buy the things the local shopkeepers in the suburbs or in your small village could not possibly keep in stock, anything expensive or hard-wearing or, on the contrary, anything subject to changing fashion. It must have been like a festival, having so much to choose from. An exciting thought, the evening before – tomorrow I will go to the city – and the evening afterwards, the memory of everything that was there.

Madrid's best confectioners positioned themselves near the Sol a long time ago. El Horno del Pozo and El Riojano still serve their *Panecillos de San Antón*, their *Bartolillos* and their *Yemas de Santa Teresa*, made of sugared egg yolks. There is a saint for every sweet sin. They let the coffee machines steam and bang, they make beautiful parcels for their delicacies in wrapping paper designed a long time ago and never redesigned, they count the money on the counters made of worn-out marble. They are still always busy. But there is more bustle in the brightly-lit newcomers selling sandwiches and CDs, beer and trousers; in the department stores invariably announcing special offers that have nothing to do with a saint's day; in the restaurants whose name and signage change faster than the menu. Because even around this square, where so much of the old Madrid has been preserved, what used to be special is losing the battle against what is everywhere available, the commonplace. Every year a couple of small shopkeepers shut down and make way for a chain store, whose trademark can be found elsewhere, attached to exactly the same articles, whether it is shoes or hamburgers. This is not just change, the old making place for the new, the inevitable rise and fall of all things. This goes far deeper.

The masses of people who used to flock to the heart of the city came for something that was only available here. Apparently there is no such need anymore. They now find something that has no special connection to this place or this point in time. But in that case, it cannot leave a memory, I think. In that case, it does not have a taste. In that case, all these people are on their way to everything and therefore to nothing. Talking animatedly they pass the old-fashioned shops with their window displays, which never change, which never have a sale and which are only carefully dusted every now and then – till one ill-fated day everything has to go, not only the display but also the stock in the drawers and the cupboards, the basement and the supply rooms, sold at prices that hurt when they are struck on the till, rattling as if it is full of little bones. On the window is written: *Liquidación total de todas las existencias por cese de negócio*. It's a sinister text, which matches exactly what I feel when reading it. But I too am only looking, as long as I still can, at this reassuring landscapes of hats and fabrics, of scissors and preserved foods, and at the old salesmen and women who are silently waiting for customers (they never speak with one another, they never sit down, they stand behind the counter and stare at the door but probably see something else entirely, in any case not me). I look and I am happy that I can, but I do not go inside and I do not buy anything.

Am I allowed to be so nostalgic? Especially about traditions which are not my own, memories belonging to other people, in a city that is not my own? The author André

Aciman, who grew up in Alexandria and in Rome, asked himself this question when he caught himself lamenting intensely over the vanishing of each grocery shop and barber, each neighbourhood restaurant that closed down or even changed its name in New York. And he answered that these small changes simply confronted him with his own sense of displacement and temporariness. They reminded him of what he feared the most: not only that he does not stand firm in his shoes but also that the ground under his feet is not solid, so that his attempts to find a new home elsewhere are always bound to fail. The exile, he writes in his book *False Papers*, experiences every change like he experiences time, memory, love, fear and beauty: always with a touch of loss. He dreams about Alexandria when he is in New York, but knows Alexandria is no longer his Alexandria and knows he will miss New York there. He passes a hard judgement on himself: not to be able to let go is the same thing as being unable to accept something when it is given to you. He writes that his biggest fear is life in the bright light of the midday sun, without the shadow of the future or the past. I felt caught when I read that. But at the same time I thought: one moment without a sense of time, an eternity between life and death, I am not scared of that at all. It is actually what I long for.

9

Food brings body and soul together. I was rich and Lhardy had survived in this neighbourhood even though so much had changed in a hundred and sixty years. I bravely turned back into the street of Saint Hieronymus.

I passed another Museo del Jamón, which suddenly seemed as tasteless as the rest of the square. A little later I stood once again before the entrance of the monument. The porter held the door open for me. My footsteps sounded in the hallway. The stairs creaked. The parquet creaked. Even the waiters' shoes softly creaked. Barely audibly. It all gave a distinct impression of great solidity. I stood at the entrance of the large, dim drawing room, panelled, draped with heavy tapestries and furnished in a timeless non-style, perhaps the way a French decorator would design an English interior, or maybe exactly the opposite. There were hunting scenes on the walls no doubt, though I could not make them out. Almost all the tables were occupied: men in dark suits, the older ones with small moustaches and combed-back hair, the younger ones with broad ties. Subdued conversations. I stood at the entrance waiting. The staff walked past me without noticing me.

It took a few minutes before someone took pity on me, found my foreign name on a list and decoded it. I was led to a side-room. It was a small room, with a few laid tables but other than that completely deserted. The man who had brought me showed me to my seat and moved away again. I was alone and it was quiet. For a second a thought shot through my mind that I would shortly be interrogated about the purpose of my visit, before being led, politely but firmly, to the exit, a serious waiter standing on either side of my shamed self.

Nonsense, of course. After a short pause a new member of staff arrived and the service turned out to be not just friendly but perfect, just as perfect as the surroundings, as the table-linen and the silver, as the bread and the oil which were placed in front of me. The menu offered a refined choice of timeless dishes, Chateaubriand and salmon and foie gras, but in the heart of the menu shone, framed, the two traditional specialities: *Callos. Cocido.* I chose the second. The waiter advised against a starter. The *cocido madrileño* is soup and meat and vegetable in one. In Lhardy they are more or less served as separate courses. I let myself be guided. For some considerable time the waiter's friendly attentions were the only things breaking the silence in my lonely room. The soup was tasty but not very special. Then another person entered the room, a gentleman in a sweater. Next, two young men who were going to talk about a plan for a film. A quarter of an hour later all the tables around me were occupied and I did not feel an exile any longer, or no more than half.

⌢

Cocido is a dish without a recipe. Each region in Spain has its own version and often its own name, which does not refer to the ingredients but to the way of cooking or to the type of pan used. It is assumed that you know the contents because in each case they are the most common products of the region. The *cocido* in Castilia, the *pote* in Asturia and Galicia, the *puchero* in Andalusia, the *escudella* in Catalonia – they all go back to the *olla podrida* which in its turn, according to culinary historians, stems from the *adafina*, the meal the Spanish Jews made on Friday before nightfall and put on a smouldering fire to eat a day later. They were not allowed to work on the Sabbath and so were not allowed to light the stove. For an evening, a night and a morning the houses must have smelled of the simmering stew of peas, beans, beef, chicken and hard-boiled eggs, sometimes finished off with a handful of prunes. The smell of the approaching day of rest, of a festive meal with the family.

The Sephardic Jews carried the memory of that smell with them to Morocco, to Algeria, to all their other places of exile. They left the recipe and the ingredients behind in Spain. According to legend they kept the keys of their houses in Seville, Granada and Toledo for generations. They were passed on from father to son, together with stories about the lost land of Sepharad, the Jews' name for Spain. A key in your hand, which no longer fits any lock, of a house that perhaps no longer exists or in which other people live – it is infinitely sad and a story that shall have to be told time and again. The Sabbath meal would have tasted different in the new country. The Catholic Spaniards, and naturally those wanting to prove that they had become Catholic, took possession of the pots and filled the *adafina* with pork. Not only cuts of meat and joints, but also sausages and black pudding. According to the food laws, black pudding with pork is doubly forbidden. If the houses were still there, they would smell very different now. Has my desire to link everything together into some religious schema run away with me? Did Jewish cooking really have so much influence on everyone else, the overwhelming majority of the population? Or is this one-pot dish simply the expedient of any poor household, which has only one fireplace and one pot to hang over it? It's a plausible thought, but an unsatisfying one. Poverty here is poor in meaning as well, and I don't like that.

∽

The waiter took the soup away and put a plate of chickpeas and cabbage on the table. The peas, *garbanzos*, form the basis of the *cocido madrileño*, the local version, which calls itself the best *cocido* of Spain, because, after all, Madrid is the capital. It is peas here; it is beans elsewhere. A simple ingredient around which a real cult exists. I am susceptible to cults, and, besides, I love *garbanzos*. Raw they look like wrinkled old women's heads but after a night in water – according to the *madrileños* this can only be water from the wells around their city – they become round and full with firm meat beneath a tight skin that does not wrinkle even after hours of cooking. It is surprising how important that first touch with lips and teeth is. It is difficult to distinguish from what comes immediately afterwards, namely the tasting with the taste buds, and what happened just before, the smell, just as it is difficult entirely to distinguish between form and content.

My waiter proceeded to serve the meat. On the bed of cabbage and *garbanzos* he laid chicken, mincemeat, *chorizo*, *morcilla* and *butifarra*: exactly the same food that had lain in glory in the packed shop window of El Brillante, and prepared in exactly the same manner. Perhaps a little drier. My friend the waiter advised me to use a few drops of vinegar.

The *cocido* is a dish without a recipe: not only because of the variations arising from the differing soils and climates of the various regions, but also because of the difference between the tables of the rich and the poor. Most Spanish kings were very fond of the *cocido madrileño*. Menus preserved from the 16th century give the impression that the *garbanzos*, or *gabrieles* as they are affectionately called in Madrid, were hidden under an extraordinary quantity of miscellaneous poultry – chicken, turkeys, doves – as well as hare, cows' tails, pigs' trotters and sausages in all shapes and sizes. Meanwhile, in the orphanage, chickpea soup was served with an egg and with only the slightest hint of bacon, which had to stay in the pot for the next day's meal. The *cocido madrileño* fits every budget and can be expanded or simplified as you wish. It has always reflected the consumer's prosperity, more clearly than a change of dish would do, but the basis remains a plate of large, white or yellow peas, barely seasoned and prepared in the simplest of fashions.

This resemblance between the food of the very poor and the very rich does not mean that the classes were close together. On the contrary: the gap between rich and poor was in Spain for such a long time unbridgeable that the most wealthy could afford to have simple tastes. Those with a plain style make clear in a subtle but effective way that they do not doubt for one moment that the gap will last forever. A well-known myth tells us that the consumption of *garbanzos* over the centuries is responsible for Spain's bloody insurrections and civil wars, because uncooked they are as hard as bullets. Since the return of democracy, interest in international cuisine in Madrid has of course been growing.

'Some more *morcilla*? *Butifarra*? Or *chorizo*?' I had almost finished, but I could not resist the sweet taste of *morcilla*. How I had changed in the past hour, how wonderful and content I now felt.

'We make all the sausages ourselves, in house,' said the waiter as he served me the black pudding.

'From your own pigs?' I asked.

'From our own slaughterhouse.'

Cocido Madrileño

Chickpea Soup or Stew from Madrid

A cocido *is served in three parts, named after the ranking of pieces in chess:* sota, caballo y rey *(pawn, knight and king). In other words: first the stock, then the peas with the vegetables and finally the meat. The vegetables and meat are also often served at the same time. You need to begin preparing the* cocido *a day in advance. The chickpeas should be soaked in water overnight and the meat boiled. The rest of the* cocido *can be made the following day.*

4–6 servings
500 g chickpeas
2 chicken legs
1 kg beef steak, in one piece
125 g smoked bacon
250 g chorizo (spicy sausage)
250 g morcilla (black pudding)
125 g smoked Serrano ham, in one piece
2 pork bones or beef bones

salt, freshly ground pepper
1 onion, peeled and cut in half
1 leek, thinly sliced
2 garlic cloves, peeled
2 carrots, thinly sliced
4 (new) potatoes, peeled and diced
optional: vermicelli

Dumplings
2 eggs
1 sliced garlic clove
1 tbsp chopped parsley
salt, pepper and bread crumbs

Cabbage
half a white cabbage, cut in large pieces
2 tbsp finely chopped onion
1 finely chopped garlic clove
salt, pepper and olive oil

On the first day soak the chickpeas in cold salted water. Put the chicken, the beef, the bacon, the chorizo, *the* morcilla, *the ham and the bones in a large soup pan with ample water, salt and pepper. Bring to the boil. Skim off the froth with a spoon. Leave to simmer for an hour and a half. Allow to cool. Next day, skim off the congealed fat from the soup. Drain the chickpeas and put them on the heat in with the meat and the soup. It is best to cook the chickpeas in a string bag or in a cheesecloth, so that they can be easily removed later, but ensuring that you can test whether they are done or not. Add the onion, leek, carrot, garlic and diced potatoes. Season to taste and simmer for an hour.*

For the dumplings: remove some beef and bacon from the pan. Blend in a food processor with the 2 eggs, garlic, parsley, salt, pepper, two tbsp of liquid from the pan and ample breadcrumbs until you can form the mixture into dumplings. Fry in oil until golden brown and add to the soup, which will simmer for another hour and a half with the lid on top, or until the chickpeas are done.

To prepare the cabbage: heat some oil in a pan, add the chopped onion and garlic, add the cabbage, and season to taste. Fry the cabbage over a medium heat until done.

If you want to serve the soup with vermicelli, cook them separately in salted water. Drain. If the soup is to be served separately, add the vermicelli. (Leave some liquid behind with the meat.)

Serve the meat and vegetables on two separate plates, cutting the sausages in thick slices and arranging the vegetables in such a way that everyone can help themselves.

10

We lived in Madrid, and then we left. Saying goodbye was sad. Dismantling our flat; the removal van driving up to the front with the same driver who had brought us four years before; the expectations that had not been fulfilled;

the surprises we could never have dreamt of; everything was carefully packed. Saying goodbye was sad, but not painful. We had not been exiles and we would never become exiles either. For those who have really been exiled a visit to their homeland is almost always a disappointment, something to avoid. But we were not chased away, so we may return without pain. Even though we are not always happy about the changes taking place in the city, through our short residence we have earned the right to notice these changes and to comment on them, to inquire after the trials and tribulations of the neighbourhood, after deaths and births, prosperity and misfortune, and to rejoice about what has stayed the same. We have more of a right now than while we lived there as foreigners. After all, the street does not only belong to our history; now we are part of a chapter of the history of this street and this city. A very small part, almost invisible and almost unknown, but it does not matter, we are aware of it and proud of it. What time took away from us, memory gives back.

Some friends from that time have stayed friends and have not changed. At least not in their friendship, in the almost casual manner in which it was once offered, so that we enjoyed it even before we were aware of it and before we understood what it meant to be welcomed so naturally, and what it meant to value each others' company, even when you have not seen each other for a long time and without saying anything very weighty when you meet again. I still do not completely understand it, I have to admit, inclined as I am to make statements and find principles, to debate and analyse instead of understand, to write instead of be, to prefer complicated recipes to simple ham.

⤿

It was the first week of December, a year after we had moved back to the Netherlands. Maria and Alvaro had invited us to their cottage, a country estate on the border of Castilia and Extremadura, about 150 kilometres west of Madrid. The last stretch of the road was muddy and full of potholes. We could hardly see the contours of the land in the moonless night. The house was a low, long-drawn-out shadow in the fold of the hills. Inside a fire was burning. We sat together till late in the evening, Maria and Alvaro, Luís and Mena, who had been our neighbours in the city, and we talked about what had happened to us over the past year and about their house, which Maria's father had built and which we would come to know over the weekend: the drawing rooms and the kitchen, the front door with its strange frame of stone circles and guns, the chapel in which their daughters had been married. We went to bed late and promised each other we would get up early, because a pig was going to be slaughtered. But the night was so quiet and we were so peaceful that as one we forgot our promise.

When we finally arrived at the barn it was halfway through the morning and the animal was already dead. The weather was cold and grey, with a little rain from time to time. In my memory it seems as if it never really got light during the entire day. But perhaps that is because we spent the greater part of it in the gloom of the barn, a twilight of brown and black, of stone and wood, against which the colours of the meat and the shrill red of the *pimentón*, the paprika powder, stuck out like on one of Goya's black paintings. The barn was part of a cluttered complex of houses and stables built around and on top of a rock. Over time, dilapidated and even partly collapsed buildings had not been repaired; something new was built up against them instead. On some walls you could see through the crumbling plaster the traces of buildings that had long disappeared. On the highest part of the rock stood the hen house. Everywhere in the undulating landscape lumps and peaks of grey rock rose up out of the green hills: the remains of a game giants had once played here on a wrinkled sheet. In some rock plateaus rectangular-shaped troughs had been hacked out, probably for drinking water for cattle. Their form and size reminded me irresistibly of deserted graves.

The dead body was almost two metres long and lay near the entrance of the barn. The skin was grey and sallow. The inside was bright white and red. Two men wearing overalls stood bent over the animal, carefully boning it. After a shot through the head and a cut across the throat they had let the blood drain from the carotid artery. They had shaved the dead animal. A long cut along the stomach made it possible to open the skin on two sides like a coat. The blood, the bacon fat, the bowels and the other intestines had already been divided up into tubs and barrels. The head had been taken away to be cooked. I had the feeling I should have been there when the pig died. Not because it would have satisfied me to see the death-struggle, to hear the shrill shrieks around the yard, but because it had already become too easy to see what was left as meat rather than an animal. I would have liked to have known it. I felt guilty, and also a little cowardly.

One of the men was called Samuel. He was the farmer who ran the estate, a thickset fellow with a cheerful smile under a well-groomed moustache. The other was a member of the family or a friend, in any case someone with a lot of experience in the area of slaughtering. The large joints of meat they were now cutting out of the body were put on a wooden table to be freed from the bone and further dissected. A heavy job. The men groaned every time they heaved a piece of meat onto their shoulders to carry it to the table. They had been working for hours. Alvaro had brought beer and *aguardiente*. Everyone thought this was an excellent idea.

In the meantime three women had entered the barn. They had been busy washing the bowels, somewhere out of sight. It is a job that has to be done very carefully, no filth is allowed to stay behind in the paper-thin skin and there must be no holes. The women were wearing aprons. They began to chop the meat and the fat into even smaller pieces, after which they put it in a long wooden trough in the middle of the barn. The women worked in silence. When the trough was full, they sprinkled salt and *pimentón* over the pieces. We rolled up our sleeves. While the others took a break with another beer, a piece of bread and a bit of dry sausage, we bent over the red-white mass and turned it over and over with our hands. It glided through my fingers, warm and soft. Pretty quickly my arms were red up to the elbows. This was a heavy job as well and only three to four people at a time could stand around the trough. So we took turns and while we were waiting we became even more hungry, and being hungry made us thirsty too. Not only the beer but also the wine and the *aguardiente* were increasingly popular. We were warm. We were also more talkative. We were slowly turning into accomplices.

After all the meat had been salted and seasoned, a large table was put up. We sat on stools and crates. By now it was well into the afternoon. Near the door the men were still busy with the remains of the pig. One of our group turned a large mincer whilst the others took turns in feeding the mixture of meat, fat, salt and paprika into the lengths of intestine and, as soon as each was full, tying it tightly to form a fresh sausage. Only one lamp lit the table. It seemed dark around us. The women started telling stories. Stories about strange accidents, about marriages and their consequences, anecdotes whose point one half of the company already knew and the other half missed. Even so we laughed together. They were like those my grandmother used to tell about the time before we were born, again and again and always in the same manner, because we wanted it that way, in order to confirm that her past was to some extent also ours, to confirm that she belonged to us and we to her. With our red hands, our flushed cheeks and our hearty laughter we tried to be there with all our hearts and be part of that company. Alvaro went round with the bottles. He filled a series of sausages with a double quantity of the spicy powder, and, when the results of our work were hung out to dry in the cold rickety attic, put these in a special place. Months later we would taste why.

By late in the afternoon the work was finished. Samuel and his family carried the tables and the tools outside. In the yard they scrubbed the red wood and the greasy metal with lots of soap and buckets full of water.

Slaughters had taken place that day on other farms in the neighbourhood as well. We visited the neighbours, one kilometre and many curves in the road away. As we climbed out of the Land Rover, we saw a scene that reminded me of Bosch, Breughel and Dalí. The family living in this house had been slaughtering in the open air. It was a very large family, in which all possible generations were represented, and we were not the only ones who had decided to visit them.

Quite a large group had spread out over the area behind the house. But the two pigs that had lost their lives there had taken possession of the landscape. For want of tables and beams, the slaughterers had hung the meat and the intestines in the trees. Over there an enormous liver was dangling next to a heart and lungs. Over here a stomach hung over a thick branch, as if it were a mattress waiting to be beaten. And on the same branch sat a small child, crowing with pleasure over the family party that was now going at full tilt. On the balcony they were still cutting. One organ after another was carried out and draped over the trees. Wine went round. Loud greetings. A baby cried. Grandmothers and grandfathers quietly enjoyed the prosperity around them. The sun, which had hidden itself away all day long, went down without anyone noticing. The meat seemed unnaturally red between the bare branches, as if it were glowing. Bacon, I think now, while looking over the pictures from that strange afternoon. Francis Bacon, he is the painter missing from my list of painters: desperate, always drunk, and who died in a hotel room in Madrid.

The party in Samuel's living room was still going on when we returned later that evening. It too was full of people. Children and their friends. Labourers? Neighbours? We ate soup. After we had eaten our dinner, Samuel fetched his guitar. Alvaro filled our glasses once more and then improvised a *cante hondo*, a song of longdrawn-out tremolos and wails that told of the special things we had done that day. The company cheered and clapped its approval. Samuel played as loud as he could. Alvaro ended his song with an invitation to answer him. Suddenly everyone looked in my direction.

I sang. I have sung, though it is not really my cup of tea. I sang about the same events as Alvaro, in his language but in my own words and everyone understood them, I was sure of it, and when my turn ended, but now with the conclusion that this was a day we should never forget and should stay in our memories, everyone agreed. It would be good for us and, besides, we owed it to the pig. Later that night we even danced.

II.

A snowy night in Barcelona

1

It was February, it was 1999 and I had hoped for balmy air, an early spring, the mild climate of the Mediterranean. But it was cold in Barcelona. I had rented a small flat in Barceloneta, the former fishing district near the centre. The flat consisted of two small rooms with a cracked tiled floor. In one room was the kitchen, in the second were a table and a mattress on the floor. The flat was on the fifth floor at the top of a narrow stone staircase with deeply worn down steps.

At every bend of this staircase stood a door, dented and many times painted and then damaged again, behind which family noises could be heard, radios and televisions, a canary, or deep silence – but silence was so unusual that it was almost sinister. On the staircase it always smelled of food or of laundry.

Whenever I leaned out of my window I could see that same laundry hanging in the street, a sea of flapping textiles against a background of grey walls. Sheets, shirts, the colourful scanty pieces of clothing of small children and the embarrassing underwear of old women – a never-ending display of flags, signalling exactly the size of the families living in all these tiny rooms, their composition and how well off they were.

In that year I was writing a hopeless novel, no, a novel about a hopeless love and in this book the two lovers were to have something like a breathing space, a short holiday in which they would yield themselves to one another completely for the first time (and also the last time, but they did not know that yet). I had imagined a hotel room in a merry, exotic city. Last Tango in Barcelona. But I was alone and it was so cold that I turned on the gas burner every once in a while to warm my hands and face. I kept my pullover on at night and pulled a coat over me when I went to sleep. I felt the chilliness of the tiled floor through the mattress. I lay with my eyes open in the dark and listened to the sounds on the street, which echoed clearly against the high buildings, every step of a late passer-by clearly audible, every word clearly understood. It always took a long time before I fell asleep. I was haunted by thoughts about the man and the woman and I knew their story would not end happily, but I was not allowed to save them. I had nothing to do with those two, even though I had made them up myself. I grew a beard. I often had an empty feeling. I often thought I was hungry.

2

In the past 20 years the city council of Barcelona has succeeded in making the city more liveable. It has created open places in the overpopulated, oldest quarters and these squares have brought new light, new air and new life into the city. Old buildings have been renovated and modern buildings erected, fitting seamlessly into the old, characteristic tangle of streets of the 19th-century neighbourhoods. They have given the city a boulevard along the sea and even an artificial beach. I witnessed the official opening at the time, in 1992, the provisional completion of most of the large buildings for the duration of the Olympic Games. A magical time. August. The end of the 20th century still a long way off. The city, a warm bowl of parties, of the tension and relaxation that belong to winning and losing, the Ramblas a bed for tens of thousands of feet walking back and forth day and night, a stream of happy people between the Montjuich, with the Olympic stadium, and the sea. For three weeks I had been a sports reporter. It was a boy's dream – and that's how I felt: young, as if anything were still possible.

Barceloneta too, had been taken in hand and cleaned up at the beginning of the 1990s. The same people still lived in the blocks of flats, but the shopping streets and the squares were trying to draw tourists and visitors from the rest of the city. You could buy espresso and cappuccino in small, austerely designed cafés, with co-ordinated furniture. You could even choose from various types of beans, with added vanilla or cherry flavouring. But this was not what I wanted to do at all: to choose.

The service in these cafés was provided by beautiful and uninterested girls who did not really have time for coffee machines because they had their hands full with their radios, their CD-players and their mobile phones with which they kept in touch with girls just as uninterested and just as beautiful in similar places 100 metres away.

They easily overlooked the hollow-eyed and unshaven stranger. As they did not pay any attention to me, I was forced to make a study of them. And I did not want to do that either, certainly not so early in the morning. More than once I left such a modern coffee shop without ordering anything. The girls did not care.

Those first mornings I walked through the streets of my neighbourhood tired and irritated. I wanted to concoct my own mixture of melancholy, homelessness and cold. I wanted to be alone with my hopeless novel. It took a couple of days before I discovered a place where I did not have to say whether I preferred coffee from Brazil, Ethiopia or Indonesia, where I could get bread with *tortilla* and where I was left in peace when *I* wanted to be. But before I had discovered it I had already found another refuge.

3

Diagonally across from the front door of my temporary home was Barceloneta's market hall. From the outside it was nothing special: a not very high, neither very old nor very new building. But when you stepped through the door you were in a different world, a village within a village, where the streets and the squares did not need names because they were ruled by the colours and the scents of the vegetables, the fruit, the fish, the meat, the cheeses, the sausages and the herbs. These covered market halls can be found in all Spanish cities, the supermarkets have not yet ousted them, though someday they will. Sometimes there are tables and trestles that are emptied and stored at the end of the day, especially for the farmers offering fruit and vegetables from their own land. In a corner an old woman sits with a bag of nuts or bunches of onions. But the larger part of markets like this always consists of professional merchants who have turned their brick or concrete kiosk into a small shop, where at night the shutters are rolled down onto the counter.

When I went into the market in the morning and walked through the aisles awash with light, the butchers were still busy cutting and slicing their meat, the fishmonger was sprinkling ice on top of his fresh catch, and the greengrocer was arranging his oranges, strawberries, cabbages and tomatoes into an undulating landscape – a little paradise before the Fall. My bad mood disappeared instantly.

Of everything there was to see, I liked the grocery shops the best. In the rest of Europe shops that are proud of their 'colonial wares' have almost disappeared but in Spain the 'Ultramarinos' like to announce that their stockfish and their tea have been brought from overseas. In fact, there are even separate shops for the stockfish, where the grey-white stuff is sold in pieces and slices – the eating of stockfish was so widespread in the days when there were no refrigerators, that there are hundreds of recipes. There are of course specialists in coffee and tea, meat and herbs, delicacies and cheeses. But a good grocer offers something of everything, an answer for every wish, an alternative for every question, and that is why he is so fascinating, because he is almighty, he is the creator of a range of products of which only he knows the logic, because he, in his white or blue coat, like God, the creator, personifies this logic. A universal genius in his own cosmos.

The market in Barceloneta had many grocery shops. I slowly strolled through its alleyways and saw the cheeses originating from all regions of Spain. The simple, robust Manchego with a tread on its hard rind as if from a tire and the old Manchego Curado kept in oil without a rind. The blue Cabrales from Asturia, which is granular and as sharp as a knife, twisting in your mouth. From Galicia the soft Tetilla, which has the shape of a woman's breast and is therefore named after it. Sometimes even the rare Torta de Casar, whose inside, I knew, would flow out as soon as you cut into it, so that you could already see how it would taste on your tongue a moment later. I looked at the sausages: stone-hard *longanizas* from the Pyrenees, a fluorescent red *chorizo* from Pamplona, the black blood sausage made in Burgos, the *bull*, a smooth tongue-sausage from Catalonia and the spreadable *sobrasada* from the Balearics. Next to that showcase I saw bags of beans, invitingly open, each provided with a metal scoop, and sometimes large, round wooden boxes of sardines, like silver wheels with spokes made of fish. I especially admired the tinned foods displayed in long rows against the back of these small, packed temples or elaborately stacked in towers or pyramids to decorate the corners of the counter. Within the grocer's universe the tins form a separate galaxy, with their own language and their own symbols. In their metal skin they are more ambiguous than the food you can see unveiled. They have a tale to tell because they have a past.

The large and small tins had colourful labels showing tiny figures in traditional costume, boats and fishes, coats of arms, children playing, merry Africans and mysterious Chinese, saints and martyrs, indeed an entire panorama of a city or a country. Behind each logo I imagined a hardworking family business on a quay near the sea or in a windowless hall at the edge of a village in the mountains. A bald man with rolled-up sleeves is bent over his figures at night and has so many worries afterwards that he cannot sleep. An advertising campaign that was actually too expensive and did not work. It sounds paradoxical but there is something about tinned food that makes it more vulnerable than fresh food, which will soon be eaten. Or will not, but that is not so bad. The sight of a rotten tomato is not in the least tragic. A tin with a dent and a faded label is. It has been waiting in vain.

The pictures I studied expressed hope and expectation, pride and pretension, all feelings I could easily identify with. They were so beautiful that their buyers would perhaps like to hang them on the wall or place them in a sideboard, undamaged by the tin-opener. Sometimes then I longed for a book with a beautiful cover, which I would not have to write. But that was a morning feeling, I reminded myself, a thought that resulted only from seeing the hustle and bustle in all these stalls and booths while I had yet to get down to work.

By temperament, I prefer serving myself to being advised, I prefer the supermarket where you can hold, examine, put back and finally pay at the cash desk without saying a word to the traditional small trader who I like watching so much. After I had been strolling around the market for a quarter of an hour and had passed the same stall for the second or third time, I started to feel rather awkward. Would my behaviour not arouse suspicion? Everybody came here for a purpose: housewives filled their shopping bags, the vegetable seller and the butcher joked with their customers, the grocer complimented them on the excellent choice they had made. Only I walked past slowly and silently in my long coat. It was suspicious. By the second day I decided I had to buy something. I plumped for a tin of *pimentón* labelled 'Choricero Oro' with a picture of a boy in traditional Murcian costume, sitting on an enormous red pepper from which golden coins were flowing. *'Dulce? Picante?'* asked the grocer cheerily. I had not thought about that, because I was not going to use the contents. Spicy seemed an excellent choice to me.

Carrying my plastic bag, empty save for the lonely, small square tin, I walked to the bar, which you will find in every such market hall. I had now justified my presence. They poured me an absolutely ordinary coffee. From that day on the collection of *pimentónes* in my small kitchen on the fifth floor began to grow. Almost every morning I added a new picture. I started to stack them. It went well. Though they were of many different makes, they all had the same shape. I dreamt about a collection. An exhibition in a real museum. A 'project' for which I would visit all the small businesses in every corner of Spain, armed with pen and camera, thus baring the country's soul without too much effort. In reality I wanted nothing more than a shop of my own. When I carefully opened the lid of one of my tins and tried a pinch of the red powder, it turned out there were indeed just two tastes behind all those different pictures. Sweet and spicy. *Dulce* and *picante*. The rest was fantasy, and tragedy.

Bacalao con Samfaina
Stockfish with Vegetables

4 servings
500 g of stockfish, without skin
3 tbsp flour
250 ml olive oil
2 chopped onions
4 finely chopped garlic cloves
1 red and 1 green pepper, deseeded and finely chopped
2 aubergines, diced
2 courgettes, diced
2 ripe tomatoes, peeled and chopped
salt, pepper, a little sugar

Cut the stockfish in pieces and leave to soak in ample water for at least 24 hours. (Some recipes say 36 hours. If in doubt, ask your fishmonger.) Change the water at least twice, so that the fish desalts well. Dab the fish dry, dip the pieces in flour and fry in olive oil till golden brown. Remove from the pan and drain on paper towels.

Fry the garlic, onion and pepper in the same oil as the fish. Add the aubergines and courgettes and fry briefly. Add the tomatoes, and a splash of water if

too dry, add salt, pepper and sugar to taste. Put the
fish on top of the vegetables, and cook together until
done. Serve immediately.

4

Meanwhile my novel made slow progress. I sat at the large
table in my bedroom in front of a window placed too
high in the wall to be able to look down. I could only see
high up on the façade of the building diagonally opposite
mine and the balcony of a flat where two elderly people
lived. Sometimes a corset or a large pair of knickers was
hung out. I told myself to stay put and just carry on
writing. But I constantly got up to see what was happening in the street and because I was stiff with cold. I let the
lovers go into a hotel in the old city centre where the heat
was scorching and they could not turn off the radiator.

I tried to stay in Barceloneta as much as possible and
not to seek distraction in the city centre. It was quiet in
the off season and the restaurants were often empty. One
afternoon I was eating in a rather large establishment
whose traditional interior had inspired my confidence.
Only one other table was occupied. The food was good:
raw mussels with parsley and *salmonetes*, a small red
mullet full of bones, with firm flesh. At the other table,
at a window looking out onto a quiet street, three English
people were sitting. A married couple – the man red in
the face with a carefully trimmed white beard, the woman
small with a despondent perm – and their daughter, who
was 15 or 16 and hopelessly ugly. They were making great
efforts to wreck their holiday. To this end, the man was

drinking quantities of white wine, the slightly sparkling house white, and the more he drank, the louder he spoke: not only his holiday, but his entire life was made up of ugliness and coldness, of disappointing tourist attractions and deserted streets. It was not his fault, he was a prisoner; he felt as if the other two had locked him up.

The moment I witnessed marked the beginning of a – in his eyes justified – rebellion, a war of liberation, and at the beginning of such a revolution everything must be demolished. Those are the rules. 'I want to live,' shouted the man. 'Live! Do you understand?' As he hammered away at her with his words, the woman became smaller and smaller, only now and then squeaking an objection. She sounded like an animal in its death agony and of course that only made her attacker more bloodthirsty. The daughter tried to look the other way and in doing so caught the idle waiter's eyes, who valiantly tried to flirt courage into her. Her father shouted at her mother: 'I want respect! Respect! Respect!' This was the finale. Afterwards he caught his head in his hands and began to moan through his teeth. The sound he produced was indescribably enraged and base. The waiter tried to give me a knowing glance. He thought that among the empty tables and the empty chairs we could watch the comedy of this splitting marriage together. But I avoided his gaze. The scene at the window table represented everything that I fear most: powerlessness leading to cold-heartedness, people destroying one another because they think there is no other way. I asked for the bill and fled the restaurant. The English people ended up in my novel as well.

5

In the evening I often walked across the new boulevard and looked at the sea. Before the Olympic Games, Barceloneta was known for its fish restaurants on the beach. They were no more than little sheds, makeshift wooden structures for the summer, but popular for the cheap fresh fish they grilled or fried over small charcoal fires. Now their place has been taken by cafés with large tiled rooms and well looked-after terraces equipped with parasols. That is where I was going to eat. For a reason I did not quite understand, I stuck to the same restaurant: El Rey De La Gamba. But I did visit its various branches in turn: one night El Rey I, on another El Rey II or III.

The shrimp in Spain does not have the status of the ham but the two are comparable. He who can order shrimps, shows he is well-off and no middle-class wedding should be without them. It would be a disgrace to the father of the bride. Small shrimps do not enjoy the prestige here that they have in Western Europe. Rightly so: I have never really got much from the subtle taste they are supposed to have. Eating shrimps in Spain means wanting to see animals and taste animals. Animals with eyes, feelers, a hard shell and a soft belly from which sometimes a string of excreta seems to dangle. It was for this that I went evening after evening to the enormous white-tiled rooms of the Gamba-king, where you could have celebrated three weddings at once. Evening after evening I ordered myself a plate of ham, a bottle of wine and a plate of shrimp. The ham was soft and aromatic; the wine was a young but full-bodied red Rioja; the large shrimps had been fried in their shells, for exactly long enough and in good olive oil, with some onions and lots of garlic, and after that, just before serving, still hot, sprinkled with parsley, sea salt and pepper. I pampered myself. I licked my fingers. But something was missing. That I had a feast placed in front of me every evening was proof of my obstinacy, but it also had an aspect of helplessness. It had to do with my two lovers, who were not in a situation where they could show their feelings, who perhaps did not possess anything you could call feeling at all. Or perhaps it had to do with the city.

In Barcelona the streets are always full of people strolling. They are dancing and making music in the open air. Even the architecture seems to be there to seduce. It is a city inviting you to fall in love, with yourself, if need be. Even so, I feel more of an outsider in the merry setting of Barcelona than among the grim façades of Madrid. I know it all too well, this open, jovial atmosphere of ports. I know what it means: nothing. Amsterdam is like that too. The broad smile welcoming you, the friendly manner in which you are helped to spend your money, hides a hard and arrogant core. In reality they have no plans whatsoever to accept you into their midst as one of their own, neither the Catalan nationalists nor the regents of Amsterdam. They are far too convinced of their own bourgeois superiority for that. Both cities have the power to make a stranger feel at ease on the day of his arrival. Cheerfully he walks through the picturesque streets and feels completely at home. Years later when he leaves again, he discovers he has not made any friends.

Prostitution thrives in such cities. There is an iron logic to that too.

Gambas a la Plancha

500 g large prawns
olive oil
sea salt
garlic (optional)
2 tbsp parsley (optional)
hot paprika (optional)
lemons, sliced (optional)
2 dried hot peppers, deseeded and finely chopped
* (optional)*

Fresh shrimps taste best when briefly fried on both sides on a hot stove, with as little oil as possible, and served with some sea salt sprinkled on top.

If you are not lucky enough to get hold of freshly-caught shrimps and have to make do with boiled or frozen ones (which you can recognise by their broken feelers, amongst other things), you are well advised to add more taste. Fry 3 sliced garlic cloves, add the shrimps, spicy paprika to taste, two tbsp of parsley and a couple of lemon slices. Shake the pan thoroughly so that the shrimps mix with the herbs. Do not fry boiled shrimps too long, otherwise they become dry.

Frozen and thawed shrimps need longer to cook (they are ready when they turn an orange-red colour and have curled up). In this case add the herbs

*and garlic a little later (shortly before you turn the
shrimps over). Serve immediately, sprinkled with
some sea salt.*

*Small shrimps should be boiled, peeled and then
briefly fried in lots of olive oil, with 2 dry, finely
chopped, deseeded hot peppers and with 3 sliced
garlic cloves, served hot in small earthenware bowls.*

6

After one week the little market in Barceloneta no longer
gave me the consolation I needed. More and more often
I got up from my writing table, more and more often I
felt hungry even though I had really had enough to eat.
I needed a stronger fix. I longed for the mother of all
markets, for the Boquería, in the old city, on the Rambla
de San José. There would be more to see and I would
attract less attention, be more anonymous. I would not
have to buy tins of paprika, neither *dulce* nor *picante*.

The Boquería is a high, half-open hall with a beautiful cast-iron roof from the 19th century. The construc-
tion reminds me of an old-fashioned railway station, not
least because of the clock on the façade. If you cannot get
a kind of food here, it does not exist: that is the impression she gives, this courtesan with the pretensions of a
duchess. There is no desire that La Boquería does not
know how to satisfy. The packed grocery stores, which
form the outer ring of this market, offer delicacies from
all over the world.

Until the end of the 1990s, when the old lady was renovated, there was a simple restaurant at the back of the

hall for those who could not wait or could not cook. It made way for a chic designer restaurant, with an interesting menu that seems very Catalan but which could have been set up somewhere else, a long way from the market. This cannot be said of the two bars, Clemens and Central, which serve food and drink from early in the morning till late in the afternoon. *Tortillas*, salads, fried and deep-fried fish, steak, sausages, sophisticated *tapas*, coffee, cognac and wine – everything is rushed in and out of the pan without any pretension and served with bread covered in tomato. The customer sits on one of the stools at the draughty bar or has to stand, because it is always busy at Clemens and Central. They make magic with two gas burners. It seems as if the men behind the bar have five arms each, or eight, like the octopus they serve in the Galician style, in slices, sprinkled with olive oil and paprika.

I seldom ate anything in the Boquería. I did not allow myself, those afternoons I had escaped from my writing table. I mainly watched. Feeling guilty and greedy at the same time, I wandered among the stalls and slowly approached the heart of the market. Its heart is formed of marine animals, and it is huge. Twenty, maybe thirty fishmongers have permanent stalls here. Early in the morning and at the beginning of the afternoon crates and tubs and boxes of polystyrene foam arrive and are laid down on seas of ice. The shellfish are still alive. Even the sea urchin pouts his little mouth inwards and outwards, while the crabs wave their pincers. The fish are dead, they do not feel the cold on their smooth skin, the sapphire gurnard and the sardines, the hake with its silver flanks, the *besugo* who seems to pronounce his own name with his round mouth opened wide, a name which could mean 'kiss', because that is what is sounds like and what the mouth looks like, the rays have wings ... but no, let me not make another list, an enumeration keeping me from saying what really matters. Or betraying that I do not at all know what matters and so am trying to conjure up the essence with noisy observations. When my lonely walks led me to the heart of the market, it was not about shells and fish. I am not a food fetishist. It was about the women selling the fish, because they were the most beautiful in the market.

They were breathtaking. Without an exception they were perfectly groomed, beaming with youthful health or else heavily made up, lips bright red, cheeks and neck powdered and rouged. Their hairdos did not have a lock out of place, the hair waved to the collar of their white or blue aprons, which often provided a view of their breasts, bordered with lace. The light in the stalls seemed designed to do justice not only to the fish but also their beauty. They wore rubber gloves reaching to their elbows.

'Fishwife' is not a compliment in any language I know and the behaviour of female fishmongers is not usually regarded as elegant. But I could not imagine these goddesses scolding. Or having an unpleasant smell. Besides, fresh fish does not stink. What would it really be like to go out with one of them in the evening? Grab her around the waist, push your nose into the hollow between the cheek and the shoulder. I didn't dare to continue my fantasy any further. I was in love. I could not deny it.

Not with anyone of them in particular, but all of them in general. And hopelessly, of course.

Pulpo a Feira

One of the most popular tapas *in Galicia is sliced octopus's tentacle. In every bar freshly boiled octopuses are hung up to drain in the morning. Apart from cleaning the octopus (removing the innards, ink and the ink sack) preparation is very simple.*

1 cleaned whole octopus
onion
bay leaf
mild paprika, sea salt and olive oil

Beat the octopus's tentacles ten times firmly on the kitchen worktop to tenderise the flesh (or put the animal in the freezer for 3 days, if you are certain it has not been frozen before). Briefly submerge the tentacles in boiling water 3 times. Then cook the animal for about 2 hours in ample water with an entire onion and a bay leaf, without allowing it to boil. Hang the octopus up so that it drains well. When the tentacles have been drained, cut them into pieces with scissors. Arrange the slices on a wooden plate, sprinkle on some coarse sea salt and mild paprika and pour over a good quality extra virgin olive oil. If desired, serve with boiled potatoes and Galician white wine.

Suquet de Peix
Catalan Fish Stew

4 servings

500 g monkfish (fillet)

500 g gilthead seabream (fillet)

100 ml olive oil

250 g cleaned squid

500 g clams

2 onions, peeled and finely chopped

2 large beefsteak tomatoes, peeled and chopped in large
    pieces

half a litre of white wine

salt and pepper

3 garlic cloves, peeled

2 tbsp chopped parsley

1 tbsp ground almonds

saffron

Wash the fish, dab dry and cut into pieces. Heat
the oil in a deep pan and fry the fish briefly on both
sides. Remove from pan and put in an ovenproof
dish. Fry the squid until golden brown and add to
the fish. Boil the clams with a splash of wine till they
open and add them to the fish and squid. Sauté the
onions until transparent, add the tomatoes and cook
together. Add the rest of the white wine and some
water as necessary, season to taste, and boil down
a little. Crush the garlic, parsley and almonds in a
mortar, add some sauce and the saffron. Stir well,
add to the rest of the sauce, bring to the boil and

pour over the fish and clams. Place in a preheated
oven for about 5 minutes, or until well heated.

Boquerones en Vinagre
Marinated Anchovies

4 servings (as starter)
500 g fresh anchovies
wine vinegar
1 garlic clove, finely chopped
sea salt
some parsley (optional)

Clean the anchovies, removing the heads, intestines
and bones while making sure that the two halves are
still together at the tail. Place the anchovies neatly
on a dish, sprinkle with salt and cover with white
wine vinegar. Leave to marinate for 2 days. Pour
off the vinegar, if necessary rinse the fish down with
water, place the fish neatly side by side on a plate
(not metal) with the skin pointing downwards.
Sprinkle the boquerones with some finely chopped
garlic and parsley and pour over some vinegar. Some
recipes swear by a last layer of olive oil, but it is not
necessary for the taste. Keep in refrigerator.

7

There is a kind of restlessness that powers you, as a pendulum powers a clock, ensuring, in spite of your changing moods, or perhaps precisely driven by them, that you remain in perpetual motion. Exactly on the last day of my stay I had finished the chapter of my book that was set in Barcelona. The two lovers had been very close for a short time, because they had had the courage to admit their fear to one another. From the top of the memorial to Columbus by the harbour they had looked at the mountains and the sea, while the first spring wind carried a strange smell to them, perhaps from Africa. After that, upon their return to Amsterdam, still at the airport, I had dealt their relationship the final blow. Their break-up was definite. For characters in a novel you want the exact opposite of what you want for yourself. Writing about adversity is easier than working towards a happy ending. I had packed my suitcase and in my mind I had already said goodbye to Barceloneta and the small flat. I was satisfied, but still restless as well. I had been working and watching for about two weeks and not eaten much other than shrimps and ham in the evening. I decided to treat myself to some real food. Food that unites body and soul. I had learned the expression from my grandmother a long time ago.

I walked over the promenade, crossed the Via Laietana near the immense post office with its temple-like pillars and ended up in the narrow streets and shadows of the old city. It was dark and the cruel wind sometimes took you unpleasantly by surprise when you turned a corner. I stood still on the corner of a small, rectangular square. I was looking for Cal Pep. I had been given the address by my wife, who knows more about cooking and about Barcelona than I do. We had once had dinner together in the Passadis Del Pep, a restaurant we had discovered by accident while following – out of curiosity – a group of well-dressed gentlemen who opened a cheap aluminium door, behind which lay a narrow corridor. Nothing on this front door told you to expect a restaurant: no name, no menu, not even a lamp. But at the end of the corridor there turned out to be one of the best restaurants we had ever visited. Without being asked, the waiters brought the most exquisite food and drink the entire evening, so good that we could not stop eating and so much that we did not need any food for two days afterwards. I did not want to try and repeat this experience, especially now that I was on my own. We would try it again, because something so glorious could not be a one-off. But such an attempted repetition, and the possibility it would fail, demanded a courage I did not at that moment possess. I was looking for Cal Pep, the small, cheap brother of the Passadis, which was supposed to be nearby, and was not in fact a little brother but the original restaurant, which has been run by Señor Pep Manubens Figueres' family for decades.

I had been standing with my back towards it. After a walk round the square it suddenly came into view and I did not understand how I could have missed it, it lay there so beautifully and warmly lit on the corner of the dark square. It reminded me of Van Gogh's famous painting of the 'Café Terrace at Night', even though there were no tables and chairs outside, no stars to be seen in the sky and it was no warm summer night in Provence but an icy cold one in Catalonia. Honestly considered, it was a ridiculous thought. It must have come to me because

I had the feeling that I would be very welcome in this cheerfully-lit room, and that is what I feel when I see Van Gogh's café terrace in Arles: I am able to walk into the painting and sit at the bar all night and there is no last orders for me. Besides, my two weeks on my own had made me a little sentimental.

Cal Pep was crowded. Actually, it is always crowded, both in front of and behind the bar, which divides the restaurant in two. At the back is a small dining room, where in theory, and according to an incomprehensible booking system (under which foreigners probably stand no chance at all), you can secure one of the scarce tables, but not when you are on your own, because that would be inefficient, as well as unnecessary. I preferred to stand shoulder to shoulder with the others waiting for a place at the bar and watching what was happening behind it. There, in one long kitchen, a great number of men in white coats were doing many things at the same time on an unbelievably small surface. Communication with the customer was in the hands of a little man with a sharply-cut, knowing but friendly face and an implausibly well-developed short-term memory, probably the fruit of years of training. His greeting consisted of a short nod, which sufficed to say: I will take care of you. From the line of 20 or 30 people waiting he flawlessly chose the next candidate for a free stool each time. But it was not until you were seated that he really displayed his mild superiority. There was undoubtedly a list somewhere of the meals that were usually available. But in reality each morning Pep just decided what looked best on the market and so you had better put your fate in the hands of the major-domo and order what he suggested. Suggest is actually the wrong word. It was more like a fatherly instruction, advice given for your own good.

'Bread with tomato,' he said.

Yes, of course.

'White wine from the house?'

Yes, please.

'Anything else? *Sepia*?'

If you say so. (Actually I was just nodding.)

The bread arrived. I had watched it being toasted one piece after another and seen how afterwards one of the men had rubbed it with a tomato until the hard crust had been covered by red, almost foaming flesh. I trickled some oil on it myself. The Catalans wish to get more esteem for their culture among Europe's peoples. They spend a lot of government money and even more words on it. As far as I am concerned they should put their feet up and rely on this unique, simple but brilliant invention: this bread, *pan con tomate*. That is what I thought at the first bite. The red bread had a beautifully black edge.

Actually the wine was good too, a very young white Penedés, which was already going to my head in a pleasant way. My glass got refilled without my asking. And then the dish I had ordered was already being served: octopus with broad beans in a mild sauce. I tasted it. True, it had been cold outside and was warm inside, but I was not wearing glasses, so how was it that I saw the working men behind the bar, the people eating next to me and those who were waiting, the entire interior with its gas flames and grills and other kitchen utensils, shiny plates and shiny glasses, flashing knifes and pans black as soot – how was it that I started to see everything as if through a quickly rising mist?

My minder took away an empty plate and put down a full one. Clams with parsley and little pieces of ham; between them one small red pepper like an exclamation mark. Again that strange feeling. Was I really going to burst into tears over a plate of food? It looked a lot like it. But it was not only the food. It is never just the food that makes a meal unforgettable. It was also the surroundings and the men in their white coats. I think it is fascinating to watch someone do his job efficiently, with confident movements, concentrated; it does not really matter which trade he practises. But when on top of that people work together, without saying a word, displaying a feeling of togetherness, a knowledge that together they are stronger than each person separately, then plain emotion comes over me. The kitchen was no larger in area than the average snack bar but here they really cooked, grilled, fried and baked. In the bars of the Boquería it had looked like a couple of men worked for ten, here ten men moved around one another like accomplished dancers in just a few square metres, in an exceptionally purposeful choreography. Well, perhaps there were only six.

I spread the already half-open shells one by one and fished out the cream-coloured animals. They looked like full little handbags with two tiny, round, black buttons. Sometimes a grain of sand crushed between my teeth. I ate and thought of the old dream: to start a restaurant myself, buying food, serving, being part of the community behind as well as in front of the bar – and going to bed every night with the idea you had finished your job, really finished it, the stove clean and everything washed up, and the next day you could start all over again because what you had made had been enjoyed but also wiped out again. I thought it would make me a lot happier than writing, but I also knew it would remain a dream. I could never learn how to cook.

I was allowed to order a small plate of *pimientos de Padrón*, the major-domo nodded. *Pimientos de Padrón* are little green peppers briefly fried in oil and then served sizzling, scorched here and there, and with just some coarse sea-salt. They are named after the little harbour town in Galicia where they are grown – and apparently not in a lot of other places, because you cannot always get them at the greengrocer's. They are a delicacy not entirely without risk. Roughly one out of twenty, instead of having the pleasantly spicy taste of a characterful pepper, reveals itself in your mouth to be a violently hot pepper that sets your palate, tongue and gums ablaze. You cannot tell by appearance. If you are careful, you can smell the danger but it is not done to hold your fork under your nose each time before taking a bite. In the middle of dreaming about a totally different life I was surprised by such a terrorist. Only sugar seems to help, but that was not available, so I ate more bread, drank more water and especially more wine. After that I ordered more food, which I got, in order to ease the pain done by the stowaway and finally to forget it. Crayfish on a bed of hot, stewed onions. Fried artichoke, which you can eat in its entirety, sparkling with oil and salt.

Pan Amb Tomàquet
Bread with Tomato

firm brown bread with a hard crust
beefsteak tomatoes
extra virgin olive oil
sea salt

Toast slices of brown bread. Cut the ripe, red beefsteak tomatoes in half, and spread the flesh on the bread. Sprinkle with some sea salt and olive oil. Delicious with grilled meat, but also with anchovies, Spanish ham, sausage or cheese.

Almejas con Jamón
Clams with Ham

4 servings (as starter)
500 g clams
1 onion
100 g Serrano *ham in small cubes*
100 ml of dry white wine
1 chilli pepper
parsley

Wash the clams, removing the sand and picking out the broken ones. Fry the finely chopped onion together with the hot chilli pepper in olive oil (do not cut the chilli open or the dish will become too spicy). Add

the hard clams, a splash of white wine, the cubed
Serrano ham and the finely chopped parsley. Put the
lid on the pan. Simmer over a high heat, shaking the
pan from time to time, till the shells are open.

Pimientos de Padrón

Pimientos de Padrón *are small, aromatic green
peppers, usually with a mild taste. Some, however,
can be extremely hot. The preparation is simple: fry
in hot oil until they are soft and wrinkly. Leave to
drain on a kitchen towel, sprinkle with sea salt and
serve as hot as possible.*

Langostinas con Cebollas Estofadas
Crayfish with Stewed Onions

4 servings (as starter)
500 g crayfish
2 large onions
100 ml fish stock
olive oil
bay leaf
sea salt
spicy paprika

*Make a slash in the belly of the crayfish with a sharp
knife, so that they are easier to peel afterwards. Boil
the crayfish in ample water with a bay leaf till they
are done. Drain.*

*Cut the onions into rings, and sauté them in
some olive oil over a low heat, adding a splash of*

stock and a pinch of spicy paprika. Boil down over a
low heat, stirring constantly. Finally, add some sea
salt if desired. Serve the onions piping hot, with the
crayfish on top with the heads pointing in the same
direction.

It was around midnight by the time I had drunk my second cup of coffee and second cognac and paid. I was one of the last customers, and they were cleaning and tidying. Cal Pep was not entirely like the café in Arles, but I found it difficult to leave. For almost three hours I had been sitting inconspicuously in a corner of the bar, eating, drinking and watching and still it was the first time since I had arrived in Barcelona that I had not felt like a stranger. Now I had to leave and go in the morning to the airport, and away.

The square was dark; there were hardly any street lamps. Black façades against a deep blue night. I took a deep breath and my breath made little clouds in the air. I suddenly had to think about one summer, a long time ago, when I had followed the bullfights in Madrid for a month. The most beautiful fight had taken place in horrible rain, the sky was clouded over, the bull and the young bullfighter had been revolving around one another for minutes while the water splashed and mixed with the blood. It was not cruel, it was moving. It was not about death but about love. The moment the boy, who was tall and lean and called Finito de Cordoba, received his applause in the middle of the big and muddy arena, it stopped raining. And while the bull was being dragged to the exit by a team of horses, a dazzling rainbow appeared directly above the arena. I did not mention this in my report of the fight. It would have been too beautiful, too much. Nobody would have believed it. But something similar happened to me that night.

I was standing on the edge of the square, the happiness of the past hours still in my head and in my stomach and suddenly the whole sky was full of white flakes. It was snowing. It was snowing silently and heavily. But even though the flakes were thick, they melted as soon as they touched the ground. No proof remained of what I saw.

Snow in Barcelona. Nobody would believe me. It was as unreal as tears in a restaurant over a plate of food. No one would believe me, and I did not mind at all.

III.

At home in Teverga

1

In the late afternoon we arrive.

We took the coastal road: Bilbao, Laredo, Santander. We made slow progress, the road was winding and hilly, but it did not matter. Thus we gradually glided into our new world, driving more slowly all the time. We adapted to the landscape of the north, a landscape green and wet and full of mountains.

We enjoyed all this greenery, but also what the people did in it, or rather no longer did, but what they had left in it when they disappeared somewhere else, or nowhere. This is one of the biggest differences between the north-west and the south of Europe: in the south, ruins survive. The countryside preserves the memory of human endeavour. You find it in France, south of Paris, not along the motorways but along the alternative routes, and even more, as you approach the villages in the more thinly populated departments, which have fewer and fewer inhabitants each year. You find it in Spain, throughout the countryside: dilapidated factories, dismantled hotels, deserted houses and farms, not sold, not rebuilt, not demolished, just left to their own devices after the owner has lost heart or his life (the heirs have already forgotten their property) or just started anew a bit further on.

In our country we tidy and clean up. Our sense of meaning and order requires it. Traces from the past are thoroughly wiped out or thoroughly restored – which comes to the same thing, more or less. Here, nature takes over a building, slowly, because nature is not in a hurry, she works with dust, with roots, with wind and rain, with branches and leaves and finally with her gravity, while rusty signs still advertise the hospitality of an empty bar and the chairs of the day labourer still stand around his table. There is no particular intention behind this phenomenon, not a human one anyway, just an excess of space, which makes time pass more slowly here. But we are grateful for it. Our journey told stories, which we retold to each other. That was another reason to drive more slowly. Rain and sunshine took turns, as if there were not already enough variety around us. As the afternoon wore on, the rain won.

In Cantabria and in Asturia we had seen houses in tropical colours lining the road: white, pink and pale green. They had verandas, supported by slim columns and flanked by tall palm trees, but the windows were often empty or broken. They stood out strangely against the low farmhouses made of dark natural stones and the labourers' cottages of concrete. These palaces had been built by emigrants who had spent half their lives in South America before finally returning to die in the place where they were born. They were called 'Indians', the returned emigrants, and of course they could never entirely return.

We saw the cold ocean. The coves. The beaches. Estu-aries where fishing boats were sleeping on the tide. On the back seat the children, pointing excitedly. Then inland. Past Oviedo, the cathedral's tower in the distance. Hills with small fields and reddish-brown cattle. Higher mountains. Bare rocks and deep gorges in which the sun did not shine anymore. The road followed the path of a stream, foaming wildly against its banks.

Finally, the tension of the last curve. The inclination to drive even more slowly, the engine turned off, foot lifted from the pedal. And there it is: the house. The windows are open. There is a gentle rain, which makes hardly any noise, and a white mist hangs over the mountaintops. There is not a breath of wind. In the large kitchen a tap is dripping, on the table someone has placed a bottle of wine. We are being expected, even though there is no one there to greet us. It is late in the afternoon and we have arrived after a long journey.

The house is not really a house. It is a castle, with turrets, cellars, a coach house and stables, a park, a chapel with a bell, a pond with an island and a man-sized doll with a coat of mail and a harness in the cellar. But I find it difficult to say 'castle', or, still more so, the Spanish word *palacio* – and it is difficult to believe we will be living here for two months. Self-consciously we unpack our suitcases. We decide which of the many rooms to sleep in. I drive to the village and find a butcher who opens his shop just for me, ask for two large steaks and get exactly one kilo. An hour later we are sitting at the large kitchen table, a small circle of light in the dark house, eating fried onions, bread and a great quantity of meat. We have arrived. It has grown dark outside. The children are sleeping, their tiny breath quiet under the high ceilings. In the park an owl is hooting. The rain is still rustling. Food brings body and soul together. Two months seem like forever.

2

The following day it is no longer raining and we see our surroundings in all their splendour. Behind our castle a massive cliff rises into the sky, impossible to scale, its peak still in the clouds. To the front we look out onto the narrow valley, with a bridge over the stream, steep pastureland where horses and cows are grazing, against a backdrop of tree-covered mountain ridges, the impenetrable wall of the Cantabrian mountains, which separate the Atlantic coast from the yellowish-brown and red Castilian plain. A landscape with so much variety that everywhere the eye and the heart find anchor points for memories, real ones and made-up ones. I choose as a study a turret room with a view out onto that landscape, drag a table upstairs and place it in front of the balcony windows. But I am far too excited to be able to work, far too happy.

It is already June but the summer has not yet started. Rainy days follow days that are surprisingly warm. Whereas Madrid and Seville have already for weeks been sighing in the oppressive heat, springtime here is often very cool. It is the price you pay for so much green and, though some people, especially those in power, might wish it were different, it is the reason why no charter flights transport tourists here for a two-week knees-up, sunshine included. We came here for the first time more than ten years ago, as guests of the family that sometimes lives in the castle during the summer. Then we came from Madrid, across the pass thick with snow in winter. From the bare peaks we plunged down into the foliage, suddenly surrounded by a fragrant world of flowers, grass and herbs, winding along a narrow road trying to avoid the potholes as we descended.

The roads to Teverga have been considerably improved since then: asphalted, widened, provided with tunnels on the sharpest and narrowest corners. New signposts have been put up. The caves in the mountains have been made accessible to walkers. In some places there is a building with the sign *Información Turística*, but it is usually closed. All these changes have been paid for with money from European funds and to compensate for the fact that the only business providing prosperity for centuries, mining, has gone. On the walls in San Martín, the village that functions as the region's capital, you can still see slogans pleading to save the mines. But alongside the roads leading into the mountains the entrances to the shafts are already overgrown, the little railways have become invisible, the towers have turned into sculptures of rust-coloured steel and disintegrated concrete. Now holidaymakers have to bring new prosperity, but for the time being there are just a handful of cyclists using the new cycle paths to cross over the mountains at the weekend. Not enough to bring wealth or to provide jobs for the men who sit on benches and stare into the main street, men whose end is already visible from the start. Not enough to reopen the shops that have closed.

On our first morning we walk through the village to see what has changed. We have happy memories of Casa Laureano, the best restaurant in the village, and of Mari, who is its cook. To our surprise, the feeling is mutual. It has been more than ten years, but she hugs and kisses us, as if we were friends or family, as if we belonged here.

3

In all the years we travelled through Spain, we dreamt of a place to stay. In the north, the south, on the plain, in the mountains, in the ugliest backwaters we studied the shop windows of estate agents. We stopped on deserted roads and walked through overgrown gardens, we broke into the ruins of labourer's cottages and country houses, of collapsed mills and abandoned farmhouses. We made calculations for the repair of dozens of roofs, for putting in wiring, for the days it would take to restore the gardens. We dreamt especially about what it would be like to be at home somewhere, to return time and again, not just to be acquainted but to recognise, and be recognised, to grow older with the new environment, to see it in the changing seasons, to touch a wall and be able to think, 'I built that years ago,' or a tree and be able to say, 'I planted that!' When you are so much in love with a country as we are, then should you not be able to find, somewhere in such a huge area, a piece of land and a roof?

There were always objections, practical and existential ones. The distance to the next village – either too far away or too close. A view that was less beautiful than we had dreamed of. A road running too near the house. And of course the thought that somewhere else there was an even better place, a spot we had yet to discover, perhaps even round the next corner. It was obvious: we were able to choose, but choosing does not belong to feeling at home, feeling at home means you do not have to choose. And perhaps it was because we were not willing or able to give up our other life, our life in the Netherlands. It is not unthinkable in principle: I come from a family of emigrants. My brothers left the Netherlands a long time ago and their children do not even speak Dutch. But did we have the courage to decide that our children would be at home in the Spanish language? Were we prepared for such a decision?

In Dutch the country you are born in is called *vaderland* (fatherland), perhaps to indicate that you have nothing to say about your emotional connection with it. It is a legal matter. In German, alongside *Vaterland* (fatherland) – a word which tastes not only of lawbooks but also of statemanship, of trumpets and drum rolls, of the trappings of History – there is the softer *Heimat* (home), which denotes love for an environment, a landscape, tastes and colours. *Heimat* is a sentimental painting, green hills, a cowherd returning to the barn, the angelus bell sounding in the distance. It may be kitsch, like every archetype in its pure form, but when I make fun of it, I do so to disguise the fact that I am touched by it. And then there is also *Wahlheimat* (the home you choose), the place which you identify with as if you had lived there in the past, as if you could choose to be born again there, Arcadia, the country where the lemons bloom, the answer to homesickness and wanderlust at the same time. I am afraid it is a utopian dream. I don't believe in it. But why does everything around me here resemble those paintings so much?

This is what I think about in the first restless days in Teverga, while clouds and sunshine follow one after the other; while the rain pours and I watch the people in the village who are living in this paradise without having chosen it, who were born here and are not happy, not all of them anyway; while I hear new stories every day about small and large family tragedies, illnesses, violence, suicides, rows and feuds, the toiling on the earth and under the ground; while I pace between my perfect study and the other rooms in the big house, not writing a single word.

The house guides my thoughts, packed as it is with old furniture, paintings on all the walls, mirrors, clocks, tapestries, stuffed animals, boxes full of letters, painted portraits, bronze busts and photographs in leather albums showing you what is was like thirty, fifty, eighty years ago. I look at the people's faces in those photographs, dead for a long time, but once, while alive, the satisfied owners of all the summers in this park, and I see their dinner on the stone table, the table still standing behind the house, under the high old trees, partly collapsed and covered with moss, but other than that exactly the same, waiting for better weather and for the moment it will be cleaned and laid again by us.

I study the books in the library, the laws and the political debates of 200 and 300 years ago in their tanned bindings, the maps with reproductions – souvenirs from art tours at the end of the 19th century – hundreds of French novelettes in flowery jackets and English detective novels from the 1930s and 1940s with paper dust-jackets. Everything smells of damp and winter, of slow decay – but it is not a sad smell, it is a smell that reminds you of the time when these books were new and were read full of expectation, reminds you of fulfilled promises in all those languid afternoons in the shade of the trees. The paper has sucked it all in and returns it now, the air of a long and perfect summer, a summer not yet begun. Between the pages of a book about Cuba, the Cuba that once belonged to Spain, we find a dried flower.

I wonder why this house is so comfortable and so unapproachable at the same time. Perhaps it is the way the furniture is arranged in the drawing room. The drawing room is almost 20 metres long and opening the doors to a side-room at the end of it adds another seven. The windows look out on the lawn with the splashing fountain in front of the house. In the room there are all sorts of furniture, in different sitting areas, some with a function, like the table bearing a collection of liquor bottles, others without a recognizable purpose, like the three *bargueños* (writing boxes) or the irredeemably out-of-tune piano – but no, that carries a collection of family portraits and so it is useful in a roundabout way. The furniture is a mishmash from various other houses, no interior designer or decorator would arrange it like this, but everything has found a place and fitted itself into the whole of which it is part. It has not been planned; it has become. Might that be the secret: the artless nonchalance, the inevitability of what is given – in contrast to all our pathetic attempts to find or to create an environment, seeking a perfection which always leaves us wishing for something more?

It is a sad thought. Because if it is right, what am I doing here among other people's inheritance and memories? Impostor. Johnny No-Home. The coat of arms cut in stone above the gate and on the towers has nothing to do with me or my family. I should not be looking at these photo albums. Worse than not knowing what to do with what you have been given is to pretend that other people's past belongs to you. And still it feels good to be here.

4

'Today: snails' it says on a sign behind the bar at Laureano's. We have seen them crawling along the walls of the kitchen garden after every rain shower. Big, fat snails with brown shells. Sometimes somebody from the village asks permission to collect them and after an hour or so he walks down the path with a gunny sack full of little animals, whose shells tap against each other in the dark. For a day after their departure and sometimes even longer the network of their silvery traces stays painted on the stones warming up slowly in the pale sun. Laureano keeps his snails in metal baskets in the inner courtyard of his restaurant for more than two weeks, where they slowly starve to death, allowed to shit but not to eat. After that he boils them out of their shells, causing a grimy scum to float to the surface. He removes them from the pan of dirty water and puts them in fresh boiling water, repeating this seven times, until no more dirt is secreted. Seven times, that is what he tells us. Seven times, neither more nor less. He swears it. Perhaps in reality it is only four or six times, but that would make a poor recipe. Perhaps the walls of Jericho fell down halfway through the fifth circuit.

Snails have tiny mouths. If you pierce them with your fork, fish them out of the sauce and keep them close to your face, their heads look like those of Martians in a cartoon. They are friendly beings, with eyes on stalks, looking around in surprise at the strange world in which they have landed. The baskets in the inner courtyard, between the crates of empty bottles and the broken furniture, look like spaceships as well, I think to myself, as I eat snails at Laureano's. The snails' mouths are wide open, like a cry without any sound.

This afternoon Gonzalo, who lives in the coach house and keeps an eye on the castle together with his wife Teresa, made a casual remark about the past. We knew that during the civil war first the nationalists, then the republicans and then again the nationalists had occupied the castle. The miners of Asturias were fearsome revolutionaries and you do not have to think very hard to guess the loyalties of the castle's inhabitants. There is a signed photograph of the exiled king Alfonso XIII in the drawing room and a portrait of a young man in uniform, his face friendly and his soldier's cap at a jaunty angle, sits on the piano, with a mourning band in the national colours. We heard that a lot of furniture was stolen at the time, and in the dining room with the frescos you can still see where soldiers lit a fire. 'It was a massacre,' says Gonzalo angrily, without saying exactly who the victims and who the culprits were, or where his own family's sympathies lay. But he spent thirty years down the mines. A massacre, he says, and he uses the same word, *carnicería*, which is painted over the shop in the village street. A massacre, a butcher.

'Where?' I ask. Because I do not really want to know 'who'.

'In the drawing room,' he says. 'That's where they lay. And on the staircase.'

In the drawing room where we have a drink in the evening enjoying the silence and the view as the sun sets behind the mountains. And on the gorgeous granite staircase with the large, wide steps leading from the entrance hall to the first floor, where my children carefully climb up- and downstairs, step by step. Who would have scrubbed the blood away? The winners or the losers?

I am eating snails and obviously I do not want to know that they are screaming. Or better still: this knowledge is lost in the eating; I am wiping it from history. They are soft and crispy, seasoned with garlic. The fact that they lost their houses before they died seems too much: the symbolism is tasteless. It is one of those dirty tricks reality plays on our stories time and again – and you must eliminate them, otherwise neither of them will be successful, neither the storytelling nor life. I am eating snails and I am well aware of what they have gone through and yet I keep eating.

Is it perhaps this? Taste, smell and substance can bring something to life again, a memory. But in order for that memory to be created something must first be destroyed or killed. Eating is those two things at the same time: creating and destroying, linked together in a movement that goes up and down but which is still the same movement, like the chewing of jaws, like the millstones of life and death. You cannot avoid your past being eaten. It has to happen. Only then does it give you something back. I am finishing an entire plate of snails, perhaps half a wall, and suddenly I also understand the remark in Manuel Vázquez Montalbán's book, which has been lying on my table in front of the window in the castle for a couple of days. 'The art of cooking is an exemplary metaphor for our culture's hypocrisy,' he writes in *Contra los gourmets*, and he must know something about it because Montalbán is not only a culinary expert but also still a communist. Indeed, I would like to go even further: all meat eaters are cannibals. The worst war is civil war. It is also the only war that teaches you something about yourself which perhaps you would have preferred not to know and is therefore worth knowing, exactly for that reason.

5

There is no longer a marketplace in San Martín. In La Plaza, a village a few hundred metres away, there are poles and fences for a cattle market which used to be held once a week. La Plaza has a church dating back to the 10th century, proof that such a remote spot is the place to preserve something, precisely because it is so remote. But the grass in the marketplace is tall and they hold a market only once in the two months we are here. Nobody understands exactly why and nobody knows when the next will be. The children stroke the soft snouts of the cows and the horses. We move on to see the church, which is a miniature cloister as well, with a small inner courtyard and a colonnade so beautiful that I wish I could become a priest and be allowed to take care of it for at least one life – and then pass on this precious, concrete knowledge. The outer wall of the Colegiata bears carvings of the animals that lived in the surrounding mountains – sheep, wild boar, wolves and bears. They are still all of them there, only their image has weathered. Inside there is a mummy of one of the oldest inhabitants of our castle, which you can see in return for a few coins. 'My grandfather,' says our friend Luís jokingly. But I had rather the children did not see him, this small leathery man with sharp teeth. He would haunt them in their dreams. I had sooner they eat the cows and the horses. Or the hazelnut pie made by Sole, Laureano's sister, who runs the café you immediately run into when you enter La Plaza, the best hazelnut pie in the entire world and the best reason to walk from San Martín to La Plaza, those few 100 metres, given that you cannot become the priest of the little church.

On Sunday mornings we go to the market at Grado. We follow the road along the foaming stream, across the river at Trubia, a village made wealthy by immense arms factories, which were long fought over during the civil war, and then west through fertile land till we have reached the market place, a small town. The shops are closed. Farmers and merchants have taken over the streets of the sleepy centre. The shoes and socks do not interest us very much. Knives and handmade funnels and sieves, a little more. But our primary interest is of course the food.

There are bakers here who have specialised in the most foreign kind of bread – a stroke of luck, because Spanish bread is mostly incredibly bad. They have plaited the dough and folded it in rings and branches and used a grain which can only grow in this region, at least so they say, and perhaps they start believing it themselves, these bakers. They also have *empanadas*, filled with tuna fish and mince meat, and barbaric *bollos*, full of bacon and *chorizo*.

Naturally there are cheeses, the speciality of Asturia: Afuega'l Pitu looks like a ripe fruit and is available in white as well as red, with *pimentón*; the spicy Urbiés is so runny that it is sold in small earthenware containers to be eaten with lots of bread and wine when it is extremely cold in the mountains; the blue Cabrales stinks with a vengeance and is the pride of these regions. Asturia is the country of milk and cheese. Opposite our house in Madrid, in a shop that now sells expensive ornaments, there used to be a dairy in the 1960s where once a year a cow from Asturia arrived to give milk to the people in the city.

I buy a *chosco* at a sausage stall, a big piece of meat looking like a sausage or like rolled meat, which is unbelievably hard and with which I try everything at home before I understand that it should have been stewed for hours to lose this hardness, but by that time it is already too late and I have given it to the cats and dogs. We fill up our bags, especially with vegetables, salad, leeks and cabbage. I am not on my own, I am not an onlooker, I am here with my sweetheart and with our children, the market is not a place now to yearn and to pine away but simply a spot which is not entirely outside and not inside, the link between being away and being at home.

We spend most of our time choosing beans. Not because they are so rare or because there is such a wide variety, but because the price is so shocking. Every Spanish region has a staple food, which it cultivates and honours, nearly adores. In Asturias it is large white beans called *fabas*, or *fabes* in Asturian. When we have finally decided which ones to buy, the stallholder carefully scoops them out of their bags and hands them over with the wish that we will take good care of them. They are the basic ingredient in the local variety of stew, called *pote*, if it is a soup, or *fabada*, if it is more solid. We are going to try and prepare those two dishes ourselves, but they will never be as good as in Casa Laureano, where Mari cooks, because she is cooking and because of the enormous quantities she makes. This kind of food tastes better when it comes from a large pan. Mari cooks *fabes con almejas*, a typical restaurant dish, combining the earthy taste of the large, oval, soaked and boiled white beans with the subtle taste of clams, thus joining the coast to the interior.

Casa Laureano is not the only café-restaurant in the village and not the prettiest either. When the miners still earned money they spent it in the village and now that the mines have closed some of them have tried to earn money by opening a restaurant or a café. All in all there are quite a few for such a small area. We like going to the oldest ones: La Chabola in La Plaza and Narciso in San Martín. They both have a bar decorated with hunting trophies and in both of them hardly anything has changed. You can sit there with a glass of wine for a long time, even during the day, and listen to the rain. After you have been sitting there for a long time, you will receive some wild boar sausage without being asked, or at Narciso, a plate of hot fried bacon. Near the bridge on the far end of La Plaza is Manolo's bar. It is an ugly location, which looks out onto a building site where they are still not building anything, and the small concrete shed where Manolo stands behind the bar would not win a beauty contest. Even so, it is always busy, especially at the end of the day, and we keep returning there after our walks. Manolo helps women and children with their fishing rods: he baits the hook with a worm. He is living proof that if you have to you can make a café attractive with a strong personality rather than beer and *tapas*. On a messy shelf behind his messy bar there is a book by a novelist who comes from this valley and who has written about this valley, of course with a dedication to Manolo, and every time I see that book – it is already a little grubby at the edges but has clearly never been read – I am overcome by an unreasonable feeling: I am jealous of that writer, who knows so well where he stands, namely on that shelf, in this bar, a jealousy I am ashamed of, and of which I *should* be ashamed, says my wife.

The people are the most important thing at Laureano's as well, because it is the people who make us feel welcome and because we believe they are sincere. Of course the food is not the best nor the most sophisticated in Asturias. It just tastes as if it is, and that is what it is all about. In the café people come and go all day, villagers have a cup of coffee, look at the football pages, make an important remark we have completely forgotten a moment later or watch with half-open mouths a TV programme which they have joined halfway through and which they will leave before its end. It is a functional place, with football trophies on the wall and advertising posters and a great quantity of cigarette lighters, paper napkins, ballpoint pens and other stuff with the name of the business printed on them, because that is what Laureano loves, and apparently finds difficult to resist, just like his son, as it happens, who – for convenience's sake – is also called Laureano.

At around two o'clock in the afternoon and after nine in the evening you can go to the dining room. In order to get there you have to walk through the kitchen, which lies between the café and the restaurant, where you must talk to Mari and the other women who are cooking. We ask each other how we are, talk about the weather and look into the pans. Sometimes she takes us to the back, to one of the deep freezes, and shows us what she herself has caught during a few days spent in Galicia, her home country. She glows with pride as she points at the fat salmon and the whopping sea trout. The Teverga's little rivers are also full of fish – from the bridge you can see the small and big trout swimming – but it is not permitted to sell them in restaurants. We get them for free, instead, delivered to our back door with a satisfied smile. The entire family fishes. One evening, when we were dining out and could not find Mari in the kitchen, we asked if she was not well. Yes and no, came the answer. She caught two salmon trout in the morning and lost them again and after that she went to bed without saying a word.

The dining room itself, which we liked so much that we had forgotten what it looked like, has – to our horror – been covered in wood panelling and the ceiling turned pink. On second thoughts, it does not matter very much. Here too the TV is often on. The menu is small and rarely changes, except for the occasional specials: a fish, home-caught or not; *centollo*, a sort of lobster which the fish-monger brought that morning; *fabada* with hare – the hunters raise their glasses to us from the table next to us; or snails.

As a starter we always have the same *pastel de cabra-cho*, pâté from red scorpion fish. We talk about what we did that day, which is not much, about the small trips we have made, the tours along narrow roads to a hamlet with muddy little streets, to a Romanesque church, a view over a new mountaintop and the valley beyond. We talk about the even smaller roads we did not take, the side tracks leading to a house which must be there because of the cable branching off the main road, but which is of course invisible and no one knows if anyone still lives there, so perhaps we should have a look sometime. Because don't we still want to ... Yes, we do, but let's not have an argument now about all the reasons why not! Sometimes Laureano comes and stands by our table and tells us about his day. He tells us about a good spot to pick wild straw-berries or cherries, or a deer or a wild boar he has seen that day. Even outside the restaurant he is preoccupied by food. He talks a lot about fishing. So pass the days, and the weeks, in the long run-up to the summer.

One more image from those days. Maria. Maria who pours cider. Cider is the national drink of Asturias, of the principality and in earlier times probably also of the kingdom. Grapes do not grow here, so they grow great quantities of apples instead. In one of our castle's cellars there is a wooden press several metres high. On the floor lie dozens of empty green bottles, which used to contain home-made cider. Maria is Mari and Laureano's daughter. More than ten years ago she was a girl who always smiled whenever she turned up in her father's café and she was the inspiration for a dreamlike character in my first novel. Nowadays she visits us every morning and helps with the children. One sunny moment Maria stands in the back garden and holds up the bottle in her right hand, her arm stretched high over her head, while her left hand holds the glass vertically beneath it, her body bent like a bow in between. She lets the alcohol fall down into the glass from as high as she can, so as to add as much oxygen as possible.

'You're even better at that than your father,' I say. I have often seen him do it in his café.

'He stood me in the river with a bottle and a glass,' she says. 'I wasn't allowed to get out until I could do it.'

She hands me the glass. A wide glass. Less than two inches of foaming liquid covers the bottom. 'Finish it in one go! You have to drink it while it's white. Come on! Every last drop!'

I empty the glass while Maria is taking up position to fill the next. The fresh, sour taste stings the back of my mouth first, then washes to the front. She adopts a dancer's pose. Don't delay and don't leave any. Cider is a drink for long, warm hours.

Torta de Avellanas, a recipe by Sole
Hazelnut cake

Soledad Alvarez Hermida is Laureano's sister and the owner of the café-restaurant La Chabola in La Plaza, where she serves this superb hazelnut cake.

350 g hazelnuts
350 g sugar
18 marie biscuits
sweet sherry
12 eggs

Soak the biscuits in ample sherry until they turn into a pulp. Preferably choose a good, more expensive cream sherry. (Whatever is left over can be served with the cake.) Mix the finely chopped hazelnuts with the sugar, the eggs and the soaked biscuits. If the mixture is too dry, pour some more sherry over it. Butter a low cake tin with a diameter of 25 cm, pour in the mixture and bake in a preheated 200 °C oven for 40 minutes.

Fabada Asturiana
Stew with White Beans

4 servings
500 g of large flat white beans
oil
1 small onion
1 garlic clove
1 bunch of parsley
mild paprika
500g of lacón *(salted beef or cured side of pork)*
2 morcillas *(black pudding)*
2 chorizos *(spicy sausage)*

Soak the beans in water and salt overnight. Drain the next day, and cover with water again. Add a splash of olive oil, an entire small, peeled onion, a clove of garlic, a couple of sprigs of parsley, and a large spoonful of mild paprika. Bring to the boil and simmer gently over a low heat, the lower the heat and the longer the boiling process, the better. Add a drop of cold water every now and then and shake the pan to keep the beans from sticking to the bottom. Try not to stir because the beans will break. When they are done you can add anything you want: for a traditional fabada Asturiana, *add* chorizo, morcilla *and* lacón, *and simmer together until meat and beans are completely tender. But it tastes just as good when you add clams (washed and cleaned of sand), with 250 ml white wine and some finely chopped parsley to make a* fabes con almejas.

On one occasion hunters had shot a (in Asturia very rare) hare, which Mari stewed together with the beans. The result was delicious. Alternatively, sliced squid or mushrooms go very well with the beans. One carefully-prepared pan provides the basis for many different meals.

Pote Tevergana
Cabbage Soup

The pote *is a heavy cabbage soup made with a green Asturian cabbage that has already opened a little. Instead of this green cabbage, you may use kale or the more bitter leaves of the turnip.* Lacón *is the salted shoulder joint from the pig, which can be replaced with salted beef or cured side of pork.*

6 servings
1 kg green cabbage
250 g lacón *without bones*
250 g morcilla *(black pudding)*
250 g chorizo *(spicy sausage)*
500 g potatoes, diced
mild paprika
oil and garlic

Wash the cabbage, remove any tough stalks and finely chop the leaves. Boil the cabbage with the meat in ample water for half an hour. Add the diced potatoes. Remove the chorizo *and* morcilla *before they are done or they will fall to pieces. Fry the garlic*

and paprika in some olive oil and add to the pote.
Leave to simmer over a low heat for about 2 hours
until the soup is well done. Add salt to taste. Serve
together with the pieces of sausage and lacón. *In*
Teverga you eat the pote *without white beans. For a*
pote Asturiana *you can add boiled white beans.*

6

Two days before the day of Saint John the Baptist, the summer, like a highway robber, finally, unexpectedly makes its attack. With such power and such heat that the humidity collected in the greenery around us is not enough to cushion the blow. I worked at my table in front of the open window. I walked to the village to have dinner. I finished my dinner, a heavy *pote*, with a rice and milk pudding. I hardly know how I was able to walk back to the castle. I am now lying on my bed in a condition between sleep and waking, in a lethargy, which unmistakably belongs to the summer. Through the half-closed shutters, where the sun pierces through the dense foliage of the oak tree standing in front of the window, patches of light are thrown into the room. I am lying on my bed and I can hear the voices of the children in the garden. I think: this will be gone soon. And at the same time I think: it does not matter. I am surprised at myself, for being able to think these two things simultaneously.

I am lying on my bed and thinking of the summer, of Spain and of Ernest Hemingway, the fat one, the insecure one, the sentimental one, the man who slapped every waiter in Western and Southern Europe on the shoulders hoping they would remember his name and take him seriously. Every medium-sized town in Spain has a restaurant that calls itself traditional and has a photo on the wall showing him with second-rate artists, shabby stars of the national movies and a beaming owner. In truth, Hemingway was given to violent orgies of gluttony and drunkenness and, except for that picture, these restaurants could hardly be called traditional any more. There are also restaurants that advertise themselves with the text: 'Hemingway never ate here.' I am not very fond of him as a writer. Too much testosterone, too much pose. But I have a soft spot for the man, for exactly the same reasons.

Years ago I visited his house in Cuba, the Cuba where he managed to spear one giant swordfish after another, while, with his free hand, he treated himself to daiquiris and mojitos, drinking them the way ordinary mortals drink water or tea. His house was impressive, a bungalow on a hilltop with a swimming pool next to it and next to the swimming pool a tower in which he could retreat and write. The sun was shining, the windows stood open. You were not allowed into the house, but you could walk around it and pop your head through the windows and have a look. Easy chairs and sofas, zebra and lion skins on the floor, a rack with magazines, a battery of bottles, books everywhere, an excellent casual taste. I was jealous again. It is not difficult to win the Nobel prize if you are that lucky with yourself and your surroundings. Only on the way back from Finca Vigía, in the car, did I remember how this jovial lucky devil had ended his own life. Just out of the clinic where he had been confined for his depression, he grabbed a shotgun as soon as an opportunity presented itself and fired a cartridge into his head.

I think that deep down he knew they laughed at him, the barkeepers, the hunters, the fishermen, the restaurant owners and the toreros, whom he hoped were his friends. Those are professions with a keen instinct for the weak spots of their customers. If they did not laugh at him, they did not take him seriously at any rate, as he tried to conquer a place in their lives. It was a difficult job. He could never manage to take part in a life and write about it at the same time. The essence kept escaping him. Living and writing are mutually exclusive.

There is a book in which he seems to realise this, which is of course *Death in the Afternoon*, where he tries to explain what bullfighting is all about and why it is not a stupid and cruel entertainment, but something morally defensible – because he feels good while watching it and also after it is over, even though he is 'very sad' at the same time. It is a fat book, with a lot of technical details and full of names, places, memories, interviews, reportage and even a couple of special appendices. Actually it is far too fat, certainly for foreigners. But it ends with an odd chapter, Chapter 20, in which the writer admits in so many words that the book is a failure, insufficient, simply because it does not include 'everything'. Everything he has experienced and loves in Spain. Because everything somehow belongs together. There is no causal connection, no before and after, no opportunity and no reason, finally everything just runs its course. And then a lament follows for all the things he did not describe, a litany starting with the phrase 'If I could have made this enough of a book,' which goes on to list, over several pages, everything the book does not contain, from the sprinklers watering the grass in front of the Prado early in a Madrid morning to the way the landscape changes colour when you are coming into Valencia by train holding a rooster for a woman who is bringing it for her sister; from the smell of gunpowder to the smell of almond milk; from throwing grasshoppers for the trout under a bridge in Galicia to the sound of pipes and drums in Barco de Avila where there are storks on the houses. It is a list that makes me like him, the macho man with the beard, because he so obviously acknowledges his shortcomings, his inadequacy as a writer and as a man of the world. Hence this helpless enumeration, all these main clauses beginning with 'and', which make a text both lyrical and stammering. In the end it means nothing, his entire book, because it does not reflect life like a mirror. It is a recognition that moves me very much.

This is what I am thinking, roughly, while lying on my bed when the summer has started and I cannot and for the life of me do not want to move. And then I start thinking up a similar litany. Because if this could have been a real book, a really good book, the book I wanted to write about Spain, then it would have contained a lot more. Not only what I have heard and seen, but also how it smells and tastes and feels on my tongue.

I would have included the morning when we had just crossed the border, very early, tired after a night on the train – how we bought sweet rolls, still warm, and ate them on the strangely moon-shaped and totally deserted beach of San Sebastian.

Another morning, years later, misty, wintry, after the early mass in Padrón, where José Marie Céla was born and his aunts still live, but we only met the chatty parish priest – and in a café near the market square we saw a woman – the flesh of her upper arms wobbling with the sawing movement – struggling to cut the fat tentacles of an octopus into slices, slices which we had already seen announced on a menu on a blackboard, and in that dark bar where only the white china dishes, from which the Ribeiro was drunk, glowed, it was a Sunday morning, and the tentacles of the cooked octopus had just been boiled and hung steaming in the cold.

And of course this should not be left out either: Puebla, the restaurant in Madrid on the corner of Jorge Juan and Principe de Vergara, since disappeared, where a cranky mother always smiled at us but never at her submissive son who served us the same order year after year: chicken bones, which we called knuckles because they looked like her fingers and which were marinated in garlic.

And also: a village in the Alpujarras where there was not a restaurant in sight but instead a woman who was prepared to make *migas* in her back room, fried bread crumbs, with a slice of bacon and an egg.

And in Málaga, on the beach, the café El Tintero, where a brushwood fire was howling and waiters walked past the tables to praise their food – 'I have *sepia*, delicious *sepia*,' '*Calamares* here,' '*Chipirones, chipirones*, who will help me out?' – and where at the end of the

Sunday afternoon, which we had prolonged as much as we possibly could, the waiter who handled the money counted the empty plates on your table and wrote the bill on the table cloth.

I wish I could tell you of a magical night full of processions in Seville: the sound of batons on wood as the bearers start walking again, the sound of shuffling feet, the sound of car tyres squeaking on spilt wax – then a sherry in little water glasses and fish fried in sour dough on a square in Triana, as the sun is nearly setting again and our eyes are almost closed with happiness and lack of sleep.

And of a sucking pig with a skin as crispy as parchment and eaten the way it should be done in Segovia: in sight of the aqueduct.

Pulpo en su tinta in Bilbao, with rice soaking up the ink next to it, so that afterwards we could stick out black tongues at each other.

And a bowl of *necoras* (spider crabs), looking like little elephant legs, and razor shells and other *fruits de mer* served on a bed of seaweed in Das Meigas, in the Calle Barbieri where it was always very noisy.

And this would have to be in my book: *leche frita* fried milk, at the Casa Poli, also in Madrid.

And in Vinarós where at five o'clock the last ships rush into the harbour and put their boxes of writhing fish on the quay – first we watched them round the jetty, then we walked ahead to the market hall to see how shortly afterwards that very fish was brought in and we bought sardines and mackerel to grill on the beach near our home.

And about the dead wild boars after the hunt with their wet moustaches, the dead bodies lying next to each other like rubbish bags – and soon the first grilled entrails and now already *orujo* or *coñac*.

Unexpectedly, as everything is always unexpected: dinner in the harbour in Castro Urdiales, where it is cold. And in Santander, where it is warm and so full that we have to rent a room in a private house, lying between the bedside tables and the wedding pictures of a marriage which is not our own but given a hundred different circumstances could have been ours too: a steaming *paella* between the crates and the fishermen hosing down their decks.

And then that night when we were driving to Val de Cabras, also at the beginning of a summer, the branches scraping our windows on the narrow mountain road and the air full of sweet herbs – I do not even know what we got for dinner in the small spa hotel, peas out of a tin I think, but even they have an unsurpassable richness in the mouth of my memory.

Casa Puebla's Pollo al Ajillo
Chicken with Garlic

2 servings
500 g of chicken portions on the bone
4 garlic cloves
100 ml Manzanilla, dry sherry
salt and oil

Deep-fry the chicken until golden brown. Heat a little oil in a frying pan and fry the sliced garlic

cloves until they are light brown. Pour 100 ml
sherry over the garlic, turn up the heat, add the
chicken, flavour with salt and reduce, stirring
occasionally, until there is a little sauce left. Serve
immediately.

Migas
Toasted Bread Crumbs

*Migas, bread crumbs, is the ideal recipe for using
up leftovers of stale, brown bread. In the absence
of brown bread, you can use a baguette, but it is
important to use stale bread for this traditional
shepherd's recipe. Originally the breadcrumbs were
fried in lard and brightened up with whatever was
available: grapes or sausages, paprika, egg or garlic.
In luxury versions simply everything is added.*

500 g stale bread
water
100 g smoked bacon
olive oil
2 garlic cloves
salt and pepper
paprika
ground cumin (optional)
1 onion, finely chopped
Also, to taste: slices of chorizo, *cubes of* Serrano *ham,
deseeded and chopped red pepper, halved white
grapes.*

Crumble the old bread (without crust, if you wish) or dice it into a bowl. Sprinkle with water, mix with your hands, until everything is a little moist, cover the bowl with a towel and leave to one side. (Some recipes swear by leaving the bread overnight.)

Heat some olive oil in a frying pan, fry the diced or sliced bacon, then remove when crispy, fry one garlic clove until golden brown and remove from the pan as well. Season the bread with salt, pepper, paprika (1 tbsp of mild powder or just a pinch of hotter powder) and some ground cumin. Fry in oil over a low heat until the bread is crispy but not brown. Meanwhile in another pan fry the finely chopped onion together with the other garlic clove, sliced, and the pepper and chorizo if desired. Add this mixture to the migas at the last moment, together with some grapes. Stir well and serve with fried eggs.

Leche Frita, Casa Poli
Fried Milk

Fried milk is made by letting a milk pudding become stiff, dicing it and then frying the pieces just before serving. At Casa Poli they flambé the diced pudding in cheap cognac, which makes it especially delicious.

1 litre milk
8 tbsp sugar
4 tbsp cornflour

1 egg
unwaxed lemon peel
cinnamon stick
flour
vegetable oil to fry
ground cinnamon and sugar

Dissolve 4 full tbsp of corn flour in some cold milk,
then add 8 tbsp of sugar, a cinnamon stick and a
piece of (unwaxed) lemon peel and the rest of the
milk. Heat the pan with this mixture until it boils,
stirring constantly with a wooden spoon. Remove
the lemon peel and the vanilla pod from the milk;
the pith can be scraped out of the stick. As soon
as the pudding is thick take off the heat and pour
into a shallow dish, so that the pudding is about 1
cm deep. Leave to cool in the refrigerator, until it
becomes solid enough to be cut into little rectangles of
approximately 2 by 4 cm. Dip the cubes in the loosely
beaten egg and some flour and fry them in hot oil
until golden brown. Drain on kitchen towel. Dip in
a mixture of sugar and cinnamon just before serving.
Leche frita *tastes best eaten lukewarm.*

I am lying on the bed, I hear my children beyond the
shutters, it is warm and I have eaten rice pudding. Now I
know why the wall around the land of Cockaigne is made
of rice pudding. The bowl appeared on the table, a bowl
with flowers and the name of Casa Laureano printed on
it, a bowl filled to the brim with sweet porridge, covered

with a pale brown, wafer-thin crust of burnt sugar. I do not like sweet things. I do not like desserts at all. So why did I eat from this bowl and even have a second helping, drink bitter coffee with it, take more than my share of the brown, burnt sugar crust, its sharp fragments? I have the feeling I know, but I do not want to think about it. Summer has come and I have found a house of sunshine and blood and rain where I cannot stay and it does not matter at all. And sure enough I start crying once more, not because of what I have seen, like in Barcelona, but for no reason. It does not matter that time passes. I am motionless myself. Without knowing it I paraphrase the great writer of the summer, Cesare Pavese, in his goodbye to life: 'No words. A gesture.'

But I cannot think of goodbyes.

Don't write. Eat.

Arroz con Leche, a recipe by Mari,
Casa Laureano
Rice pudding

4 servings
1 cup of water (125 ml)
a pinch of salt
cinnamon stick
unwaxed lemon peel
60 g butter
1 cup of short-grain rice
3 cups of sugar
1 litre (or more) full-cream milk

Heat the water, rice, salt, cinnamon stick, lemon peel (to taste) and butter in a pan. When it boils, add the milk little by little, stirring constantly and over a low heat until all the milk has been absorbed. This can take more than 2 hours. Do not add the sugar until the rice is completely done, and the substance thick but not entirely solid. Then add the sugar, simmer gently over a low heat for 15 minutes, stirring constantly. Pour the rice pudding into a large bowl. Leave to cool. Sprinkle with sugar, which you can caramelise with the same kind of blowtorch you would use for crème brûlée, or put under the grill.